The Cognitive Leader

Building Winning Organizations Through Knowledge Leadership

Roderic Hewlett

Roman & Littlefield Education
Lanham, Maryland • Toronto • Oxford
2006

Published in the United States of America
by Rowman & Littlefield Education
A Division of Rowman & Littlefield Publishers, Inc.
A wholly owned subsidary of The Rowman & Littlefield Publishing Group, Inc.
4501 Forbes Boulevard, Suite 200, Lanham, Maryland 20706
www.rowmaneducation.com

PO Box 317
Oxford
OX2 9RU, UK

British Library Cataloguing in Publication Information Available

Library of Congress Cataloging-in-Publication Data

Hewlett, Roderic, 1958–
    The cognitive leader : building winning organizations through knowledge
    leadership / Roderic Hewlett.
        p. cm.
    Includes bibliographical references and index.
    ISBN 1-57886-310-4 (hardcover : alk. paper) — ISBN 1-57886-311-2
    (pbk. : alk. paper)
    1. Knowledge management. 2. Leadership. I. Title.

HD30.2.H47 2006
658.4'038—dc22

                                                            2005018448

∞™ The paper used in this publication meets the minimum requirements
of American National Standard for Information Sciences—Permanence of
Paper for Printed Library Materials, ANSI/NISO Z39.48-1992.
Manufactured in the United States of America.

CONTENTS

ACKNOWLEDGMENTS

My most heartfelt thanks to my wife, Donna, who nurtures my ideas, edits my work, and shows unending support. I owe a tremendous debt of gratitude to my son, Ian, and daughter, Janna. Our children followed Donna and me around the world and made many sacrifices so that I might learn.

No one person is ever responsible for what that person writes. Individuals are a collection of intellectual contributions from the many people who have touched their lives. So it is with me. This book is a product of scores of wonderful leaders, colleagues, teachers, and mentors who so generously gave of their knowledge to improve mine. Thank you!

My special gratitude to William "Billy" Lee, Textron Aerostructures; Sergeant First Class Jurado, U.S. Army; Sergeant First Class Philip Bonner, U.S. Army; and Dr. Reuben Kyle, professor at Middle Tennessee State University, who were so very instrumental in my development and patient in their mentoring.

Preface

Leadership is the quintessential ingredient that sparks the organizational fire of greatness. Poor leadership can extinguish that organizational fire. Throughout history, many have sought the Holy Grail of leadership only to lose sight of their quest. Biographical sketches seek to unlock the personalities of great leaders and set into context the times of great leaders as a way to teach the principles of leadership. Walk into a library or a bookstore and you will find countless books, articles, and manuals craftily articulating the "science" of leadership. The interest in learning how to lead is huge, but is the story of leadership complete?

As global economies evolve beyond industrial- and agricultural-based societies to knowledge-based societies, organization leaders are scrambling to understand how to use knowledge to compete, fulfill their mission, and create value. The new knowledge societies and organizations that form the backbone of the 21st-century organization create new leadership challenges. Leading cognitive or "metaphysical" organizations presents new challenges to the aspiring leader.

Leaders are challenged to articulate, what is knowledge? How can knowledge be used to create value? How can leaders adapt to effectively lead organizations that create "intangible products"? What type of knowledge does an organization need to succeed and how can it be measured? How do humans fit into the new organizational equation? All of these important questions highlight the leadership dilemma of the 21st century.

Thought—or cognitive—leadership requires thoughtful leaders. The bold new world of knowledge capitalism has emerged and the new cognitive leader must prepare to harness this new form of capitalism. Open the pages and begin the quest to be a masterful cognitive leader.

ONE

THE KNOWLEDGE LEADER

You have real evolution only under freedom. . . . What you get in unfree systems is due to the fact that the emergence of the better has been prevented.

—Friedrick A. von Hayek

The precision flying maneuvers exhibited by migrating birds in formation should make any leader jealous. How can these creatures effortlessly navigate thousands of miles to pinpoint locations? The alignment and symmetry of their flight are inspiring to watch. Anyone who has attempted to orchestrate human activities for a common purpose can only watch with envy as birds innately align for a common purpose.

Humans, a cognitive species, appear to emulate stray cats more than the well-aligned flock of birds. Leading an organization often seems like herding stray cats. How can leaders ever hope to align human activities to build thriving organizations? The answer lies in understanding human nature and tapping the power of knowledge.

Nobel Prize–winning economist Friedrich Hayek's enduring life's work was an attempt to understand what made capitalism work and socialism fail (Ebenstein, 2001). Hayek made no moral distinction between these two opposing systems. He merely acknowledged that socialism failed because it was based on central planning and control, while capitalism succeeded because it tapped into human aspirations and the mechanisms of "spontaneous order" that guide human activities.

Hayek's ultimate message put forth in his final book, *The Fatal Conceit: The Errors of Socialism*, is "life has no purpose but itself" (Hayek, 1988, p. 133). Hayek's biographer Alan Ebenstein (2001) expands this statement by noting that Hayek clearly announces in the first few chapters of *The Fatal Conceit* that "the development of human life is conterminous with the development of knowledge, technology, and material creation, and that the society in which these are most developed is the best society" (p. 312).

1

Hayek knew that knowledge was distributive among humans. No individual, or group, can conceivably have all of the answers.

Hayek notes that successful organizations and societies build rules and laws that provide the least coerciveness and guide human efforts. Hayek also points out that price and profits are knowledge signals that guide human activity to the most rewarding efforts. Talent is attracted to high wages and manufacturing capability is reserved for high-return products. Hayek knew that humans need more complex signals than a flock of birds to successfully coordinate our complex cognitive activities.

Based on Hayek's guidance, why should we expect highly coercive, egocentric, and overtly directive leadership styles to produce significant and sustained results in today's knowledge-based global organizations? How can governmental leaders correctly direct the efforts of diverse government activities? How can a not-for-profit board of directors and executive officers guide the complex activities of volunteers and professional staff?

LEADERS' ROLES IN ORGANIZATIONAL SUCCESS

Leadership is the art of aligning capital and human activity to achieve desired results. During the early days of industrial capitalism, central planning and managerial control punctuated complex technical and production models. These methods worked because the human component was diminished to simple and repeatable tasks. Today, successful organizations use human knowledge to drive decision making. In the new global entrepreneurial economy, knowledge has become the clear delineating element of success. Leadership skills, communication, motivation, and planning remain the key elements of leadership. However, successful leaders also nurture and harness organizational knowledge.

LEADERSHIP ENVIRONMENT

As the inquiring leader absorbs lessons from books on leadership, a quest for the "successful leadership formula" emerges. A lesson not typically noted in the books is how the leader serves to align the relationship between organizational purpose and resources. In most cases the books are rich on theory and motivation, but they are deadly silent on building practical leadership skills that deal with the soft portions of leadership. To further complicate the daunting tasks that fall to leaders, organizational needs shift over time—there are no easy formulas. The knowledge-based leader faces a dynamic environment requiring constant adjustment.

All leaders are organizational stewards. They understand that all organizations have a blend of assets known as capital. Some of this capital is tangible, such as buildings, machines, computers, and money. These forms of capital are well-known as the physical and financial assets. Recently, non-tangible forms of capital, such as human, intellectual, and structural capital, have been added to the list of organizational capital available to leaders. Good leaders leverage capital through good decision making. Most decisions to be made are future oriented, where "facts" are unknown—they are made under conditions of uncertainty. The essence of good leadership practice is the ability to engage in decision making, foster organizational alignment, and produce results in an environment of uncertainty. Given this environment, leaders feel anxious when decisions must be made where there is a generally mushy understanding of the issues as well as the sinking feeling in their stomachs when these decisions will decide the fate of their careers. Take heart. Leaders can align decision making and organizational activities to achieve desired results by understanding the nature of leadership, employing knowledge, and using planning techniques.

GOOD LEADERSHIP CHARACTERISTICS

Good leaders have certain decision-making characteristics that increase the potential for organizational success. Good leaders seek to develop these key characteristics:

- Listening well
- Identifying key individuals to be involved in framing and informing decisions
- Working with stakeholders to develop clear goals for decision making
- Establishing the scope, timing, and context of decisions
- Developing alternative courses of actions
- Identifying knowledge required for the decisions
- Encouraging an environment of trust, respect, and openness
- Seeking results through collaboration and knowledge use—not controlling

Leadership decision-making characteristics are essentially knowledge tasks: knowledge about people, products, services, competitors, and the external environment. Knowledge informs decision makers about the dimensions of the decision process. The person who has the knowledge determines who must be involved in the decision-making process. How much knowledge we possess determines the degree of uncertainty, or risk, inherent in the decision. Knowledge dictates the quantity and quality of the courses of action available in decision making. Knowledge is central to decision making, and decision making is central to effective leadership.

COLLABORATION

Hayek's notion of distributive knowledge mandates collaboration for good decision making, but not consensus or unanimity of approval for the decision. Distributive knowledge, in Hayek's view, merely means that the knowledge to "do things" is distributed among humans—no one person knows enough to "do it" alone. The notion of distributive knowledge may seem complex; however, Hayek's view is simplicity itself—humans are interdependent. Leaders can fall into the trap of believing they must know and control everything in an organization. This unfortunate notion is based on a blatantly false belief that leaders have super endowments of knowledge and capacity. The naked truth is that effective leaders know how to link people with other organizational resources to produce results. Leaders know how to collaborate. Interestingly, some aspiring leaders confuse collaboration and consensus. Collaboration essentially lets everyone have a say and distributes ownership, whereas consensus is seeking approval from everyone.

Consensus leads to "paralysis by analysis." Developing a collaborative institutional framework that establishes "the rules" for decision making is essential. Collaboration requires an environment—established by leaders—that engenders trust and leads to engagement. Collaboration is linking individual knowledge and aspirations to organizational success. Leaders collaborate to define the "lighthouse" themes in an organization that guide individuals in their activities. Hayek's "lighthouse" concepts for guiding economic activity include the roles that prices and profits play in guiding businesses in their activities. Missions, objectives, strategies, employee development, and all organizational activities are guided by "lighthouse" concepts, and this is the key reason leaders exist. Leaders should not abrogate decision making to a group, but instead garner group members' wisdom, experiences, and acceptance. Collaboration with rules—who makes the decision and how the decision is to be made—establishes the edges of the envelope for the organization. Collaboration is a knowledge-building process—not a decision-making process.

LEADERSHIP OF ORGANIZATIONAL CAPITAL

Organizations employ capital daily. Leaders should have the knowledge to grasp the dimensions, composition, and methods of blending different forms of capital to fulfill organizational purposes.

A leader must be the catalyst within an organization in clarifying the ideal state, the achievable state, and the current state of an organization. The challenge of leadership lies in blending purpose, capital, and leverage to bridge the gap between the current state of the organization and the necessary achievable state. The leader must keep an eye focused on what it takes to attain the ideal state as well, but the leader must do so with care because the ideal may become the antithesis of the achievable. It is simple; do not break the organization in an attempt to leapfrog from the current state to the ideal state in one fell swoop.

WHAT IS KNOWLEDGE-BASED LEADERSHIP?

Simple definitions may seem elusive. But in its most basic sense, knowledge-based leadership is the unleashing of knowledge and human potential to enable the organization to be successful, manage change, and thrive. The answers to achieving organizational success are the levels and uses of knowledge teased out through good leadership. To understand knowledge-based leadership fully, it is helpful to reflect on the role of knowledge in human development.

What singular characteristic makes humans unique in the animal kingdom? Is it our physical features? Not really; many other mammals share common physical traits with humans. Can it be communication? Not completely; other species have unique ways of communicating. Then what is the singular factor that makes humans unique? The answer lies in our unique ability to think deeply and comprehensively, accumulate higher-order knowledge, and apply new knowledge to solve problems. The discovery and use of high-order knowledge is the defining characteristic that makes possible the formation of societies, advances in science that harness nature's bountiful gifts, and the creativity of the arts that enriches our lives.

A good way to view the relationship between knowledge and organizational growth is to think of it as an automobile on a trip. The four components of the automobile that are of keen importance are the engine, transmission, driver, and wheels. Knowledge is the engine of growth and transformation. The wheels represent productivity, creativity, and growth. The transmission represents human capabilities. The driver represents leadership and controls the power of all of the other components. A high-powered engine without a transmission will not move the organizational wheels of growth. All components must work in harmony to move the vehicle along the journey. Just as the key components of a vehicle are synergistic, so is knowledge-based leadership.

LEADERSHIP AND KNOWLEDGE

Global organizations change at a tremendous pace. A business ripple in China is felt by small local businesses in Montana. Consider the price of fuel for a local Montana business. As China and India continue to develop, their demand for fossil fuels affects the global supply and demand and hence prices of oil products. The Montana business owner now must pay more for local purchases of fuel based on global forces. To keep pace with this rapid change, strategy gurus argue that knowledge is central to managing the blistering pace of change (Bryant, 2003). In three key knowledge dimensions, leaders are the architects who hone an organization's knowledge capabilities: creating, sharing, and using knowledge to gain advantage. Leaders who shape knowledge use in an organization can be formal and informal leaders as well as voluntary and involuntary leaders. So everyone in an organization has the potential to be a "leader."

Knowledge is an essential building block in framing a vision as well as the development of systems, meaningful incentives, and structures that lead to organizational success. These key building blocks provide organization signals, just like prices and profits are signals for capitalists. In the past, internal and external relations were viewed as key ingredients to organizational success. In today's hypercompetitive world, organizations are challenged to do more with less. Accordingly, resources cannot form the edge of the organizational capabilities "envelope"; rather, organizations must innovate beyond traditional resource limitations. Only organizations that use knowledge effectively have the capacity to innovate, adapt, invent, and thrive. Leaders provide the context, climate, and resources for organizational innovation (Bryant, 2003).

KNOWLEDGE IS POWER

Increasingly, knowledge is the currency of success. Leadership demands, in our complex world, require leaders to draw extensively on knowledge. Clearly, economic importance in today's world is drawn into focus by what people know (Samuelson, 2004). The ability to assess risk, develop resources and competitive endowments, make valuations, and develop solid preferences are clearly tied to a leader's ability to align the "flock." Managing, or leading, in a knowledge-intensive world is clearly tied to wisdom acquisition. Mistakenly, many organizations have taken the "database path" in attempting to "catalog and store" knowledge.

To some, a technologically driven process equates to "knowledge management." Following this path can lead to a misapplication of resources and failure to acquire a knowledge advantage. To lead with knowledge, one must recognize that knowledge is not a technology issue, but technology can enable knowledge acquisition, sharing, and application. Technology can enhance the communication process, but technology cannot store knowledge or wisdom for mere retrieval and application at a later date. Knowledge and wisdom are uniquely human.

Core knowledge, which is baseline to organizational success, is evanescent—it dissipates and becomes obsolete. Leading with knowledge is complex and requires deep understanding, appreciation of the nature of knowledge, and a method to tap knowledge and use it throughout the organization. To align humans like the flock of migrating birds is daunting, but by leading with knowledge the task is achievable.

TWO

HOW KNOWLEDGE SHAPES DAILY LIFE

I like to think of thoughts as living blossoms borne by the human tree.

—James Douglas, "Down Shoe Lane"

Life would be bland if every day was a mere repeat of the previous day: no learning, no change, and no growth. Humans are constantly changing—it seems to be hardwired into our genes—accumulating knowledge from many sources and reshaping our lives through experiential and vicarious learning (Bandura, 1977). Experiences, thoughts, conversations, images, and reflections bombard us daily and learning is the result of this daily bombardment. The cumulative learning from everyday events and formal learning adds to the sum of our knowledge. Formal and informal knowledge blends to shape us. This same learning process defines organizations too. If the organization adopts a knowledge orientation and harnesses knowledge to achieve organizational objectives, then a learning organization emerges. Leaders craft the environment to foster a learning organization.

Humans are learning creatures. We are constantly learning, but what are we learning? Shaping learning is the craft of leadership. Knowledge goes almost unnoticed in many organizations; it is just there—in procedure manuals or resident with the person who has been in the organization beyond the horizon of memory. Coincidental knowledge can be dangerous for an organization since members of the organization may be learning the wrong things. Since people are constantly learning, the leader should be consumed with organization learning and how knowledge is applied to create value. Learning should focus on key elements of organizational success. One need only look at the effects of a mind-robbing disease to fully grasp how knowledge shapes an individual life. Knowledge also shapes organizations; while the symptoms of organizational disease are different, they can also destroy the organization much like the illness robs the individual. The devastating memory loss of the individual with Alzheimer's disease is a clear example of how knowledge shapes an individual's life.

The woven texture of human lives is made up strand by strand of experiences that form the fabric known as knowledge. The debilitating effects of a disease such as Alzheimer's illustrate the effects of a rip in the fabric of life causing the loss of knowledge—the effects of Alzheimer's disease on human life is devastating, and it highlights a life devoid of knowledge: knowledge of friends, family, experience, and facts. The Alzheimer's patient, unfortunately, provides a living example of the effects of knowledge on humans. Before the patient is subjected to the effects of the disease, they are full of life and rich with knowledge. Then the disease begins to ravage their brains, stripping knowledge and then life from the patient. As anyone who has watched this disease in another can attest, knowledge is life.

The tacit, or self-contained, knowledge of the Alzheimer's patient is lost as the disease progresses; however, the explicit knowledge of the patient can be retained and enjoyed indefinitely. Pictures, letters, memorandums, tapes, and the memories of family diaries carry on the knowledge legacy of the patient. There is a lesson, for the wise leader of an organization, to be learned from those who suffer the ravages of Alzheimer's: Capture and use the knowledge of everyone in the organization. Make tacit knowledge explicit for use and preservation. Knowledge is legacy.

In an organization, "disease" is manifest through high employee turnover, loss of employee motivation, reduced productivity, and loss of innovation. The knowledge of an organization, as well as the incentive to learn, is destroyed through the "disease" of poor leadership that causes a loss of knowledge. The leader assumes the ultimate responsibility to ensure that an organizational climate is established that fosters knowledge wellness. The organization is composed of knowledge assets known as people. An effective leader knows these people, not always by name, but always through understanding their aspirations, values, and how knowledge shapes their lives and ultimately the life of the organization.

KNOWLEDGE AND PERFORMANCE

The stages of life can be tracked by stages of learning and knowledge use. The first stages of life are made up of intense periods of formal education in an attempt to "jump start" our knowledge base. This early education is deemed so essential to societal well-being that in advanced societies a large proportion of spending is dedicated to formal education. In the United States, during the academic year 1959–1960 approximately $375 per student was spent for educating primary and secondary students. Adjusting the 1959–1960 per student expenditure for inflation reveals that in the fall of 2000 the spending for primary and secondary students would be $2,100 if based on the same real level of 1959–1960 per-student spending; however, the actual per-student expenditure for fall 2000 was $7,392 (*World Almanac*, 2003). Economic theory suggests that what people do with their limited resources, such as time and money, reveals their preferences. People recognize the role education plays in knowledge development and demonstrate this preference with their pocketbooks.

Subsequent stages of life also consist of knowledge acquisition, but these acquisitions are more subtle and consist of knowledge integration and growth from rudimentary levels of knowledge to more refined levels of wisdom. Some refer to these integrated forms of knowledge as "common sense." Formal education through higher education still plays a large role in the adult's knowledge acquisition strategy. In 2002, 26.7% of the population over the age of 25 in the United States held at least one bachelor's degree (Gaquin & Debrandt, 2003). Many other forms of learning exert influences on individuals during the adult years, such as on-the-job training, professional associations, career training, informal learning such as reading or documentaries, as well as hobbies. Life is about learning and knowledge use. Is this knowledge and learning phenomenon limited to the United States or is it a global phenomenon?

A recent World Bank report (1999) characterizes knowledge as the essential ingredient for proper market functions, a key variable that differentiates between rich and poor countries and defines a nation's prospects for future development. The World Bank report suggests that knowledge gaps can be caused by access to technology used to communicate knowledge. The gaps are most evident in technologically rich and poor countries. The report further suggests that developing countries must acquire three key capabilities to narrow the knowledge gaps: the abilities to acquire, absorb, and communicate knowledge. Careful consideration, and reflection on, these key three capabilities suggests that they are the key components for growth in any individual, organization, or country.

KNOWLEDGE CONTROLS DESTINY

Human history is punctuated with periods of economic growth and decay. Great societies rise and fall over the ages, but why do some last longer and others fall quickly? The answer is quite complex; however, most great societies are built on a knowledge foundation—even if it is a military knowledge foundation.

Ancient Greece, Rome, Egypt, and China are examples of zenith knowledge societies cresting Before the Common Era (BCE). These societies controlled large landmasses and dominated other regions of the world. A central thread in these arguably great ancient societies was the focus on

knowledge and sharing of knowledge. These societies had learned schol-
ars, libraries, and a system of education, laws, and philosophies. In short,
the societies possessed knowledge-based institutions that fed the arts and
sciences and created an impetus for growth.

HOW KNOWLEDGE AFFECTS ECONOMIES AND SOCIETIES

Businesses, not-for-profits, and governmental organizations also compete to grow their "bottom line." The bottom line for businesses is
straightforward—profit. For not-for-profit and governmental organizations the bottom line looks a little different. Specifically, these organizations measure success in having a positive "fund balance" so they may
successfully pursue their mission of assistance. Yet, the common denominator among all types of organizations is the successful accomplishment
of organizational mission, however it is defined, and having the necessary funds to support success. Today, all organizations compete on the
basis of knowledge—knowledge is central to mission accomplishment.

Knowledge-based products and services are key characteristics of modern global organizations. Alan Greenspan (2002), chairman of the U.S.
Federal Reserve System, made insightful comments about the role of
knowledge in spurring economic growth. Greenspan traced the role
of knowledge and education in transforming the economy of the United
States. Greenspan noted,

> Over the last century, for example, real gross domestic product in the United
> States has grown at an average of more than 3 percent per year. Only a small
> fraction of that increased value represents a rise in the tonnage of physical
> materials—oil, coal, ores, wood, and raw chemicals, for example. The re-
> mainder represents new insights into how to rearrange those physical mate-
> rials to better serve human needs.

Briefly reflect on the history of the human race. A similar view of the role
of knowledge as a catalyst for growth emerges—much as the role described by Greenspan in recent U.S. history.

OUR MODERN WORLD IS A COMPILATION OF KNOWLEDGE

Humans started their existence as hunter-gathers. Jared Diamond (1999)
in his landmark book *Guns, Germs, and Steel: The Fates of Human Societies*,
provides an excellent account of the growth and evolution of the human
race and the role that knowledge, discovery, and innovation play in that
evolution. Diamond describes the changes in humans from Java "man"—

actually a woman—dated 1.8 million years ago—to the changes about a half million years ago in Africa and Europe when Homo sapiens emerged. According to Diamond, human history became particularly exciting about 50,000 years ago in what he describes as the "Great Leap Forward."

Diamond recounts the tools and hunting weapons found in Cro-Magnon sites in southwest Europe some 40,000 years ago. These tools were fashioned out of animal bones and stones, representing, in a crude fashion, what Greenspan refers to as human knowledge influences on physical materials "to better serve human needs." Humans have always advanced when they apply knowledge to harness physical properties found on this planet. The buildings, automobiles, aircraft, technology, and medicines that we enjoy today are all knowledge-based products. The arts and humanities and other endeavors that spur greatness in humans are also knowledge based.

Interestingly, Greenspan (2002) quips, "Engineering and metallurgical insights have reduced the number of people required to produce a ton of steel, but the same number of musicians will be needed to perform a Beethoven quartet this evening as were needed a century ago." In a traditional sense, Greenspan is correct; however, knowledge has advanced technology to such a state that instruments and other sounds can be synthesized and reproduced with greater accuracy than ever before. Consider the advances in compact discs (CDs) over the old, scratchy vinyl records. The fidelity of the sound is considerably improved through knowledge and technological innovations. Enjoyment of the arts as well as the advances in the sciences are enhanced as knowledge advances the state of the art.

As knowledge supplants other ingredients in economic growth and competition, wealth will increasingly be denominated in the currency of knowledge. This knowledge trend expands from earlier epochs of capitalism. Finance and physical capital reigned supreme in garnering wealth during the Middle Ages through the early part of the 20th century (Braudel, 1977). To develop economic concentration, money and cities became linked during the Middle Ages. Economic growth followed the advances in knowledge in Renaissance and Enlightenment cities such as 15th-century Venice, 17th-century Holland, and 18th-century London. However, the returns to "knowledge" were confined to the financiers and subsequently the capitalists who employed large-scale physical capital. Beginning in the twilight of the 20th century and continuing into the 21st century, the knowledge capitalists are garnering the financial wealth. Greenspan (1999) captures this emerging truth in an address to the Gerald R. Ford Foundation:

> America's industrial might earlier this century [20th century]—large steel mills, auto assembly plants, petrochemical complexes and skyscrapers—have been replaced by a gross domestic product that has been downsized as

ideas have replaced physical bulk and effort as creators of value. Today, economic value is best symbolized by exceedingly complex, miniaturized integrated circuits and the ideas—the software—that utilize them. Most of what we currently perceive as value and wealth is intellectual and impalpable.

As knowledge increasingly serves as the foundation of wealth and economic progress, questions abound about how to manage knowledge, protect investments in knowledge, and apply knowledge in a meaningful manner.

The political founders of America understood the role of knowledge in advancing America's growth. During the writing of the U.S. Constitution, the framers wrote a provision in Article 1, Section 8 that stated, "To promote the Progress of Science and useful Arts, by securing for limited time to Authors and Inventors the exclusive Right to their respective Writings and Discoveries" (as cited in Monk, 2003, p. 52). This provision in the Constitution allows the establishment of laws to protect inventions through patents and creative works and intellectual property through copyrights. Even in the 18th century, it was well understood that knowledge was a central feature of social progress. Accordingly, there must be meaningful rights to protect incentives for innovation and creation. Most industrialized countries have copyright and patent laws. Currently, the World Trade Organization (WTO) provides monitoring and oversight of global intellectual property protections.

An active debate still rages over how effective patents are in protecting intellectual, or knowledge, rights versus the stifling of innovation by controlling others' use of the knowledge contained in the patent (Gallini, 2002). But there can be no doubt that currently there is an explosion of knowledge and creative products. Between 1985 and 1999 there was an annual growth rate of 100% in patents granted in the United States. In the 1980s, an average of about 60,000 patents was granted each year, but by the 1990s this yearly average had jumped to 150,000 per year. The knowledge embedded in patented and copywritten material abounds in libraries, online, and in various forms of media that can be purchased.

Researchers over the past few decades have questioned the effectiveness of counting patents as the key measure of innovation. Recent research suggests that a better measure than patents as proxies for innovation may be patent citations (Jaffe & Trajtenberg, 2002). Jaffe and Trajtenberg found that citation, or the number of times a patent is cited by subsequent patents, is a better measure of innovation. Simply put, patent intensity is a strong measure of useful knowledge creation. However, the absolute growth in patents remains an effective measure of growth in usable knowledge. Knowledge matters in a society and has strong implications for the economy. But the question still lingers, is knowledge more than mere data and information?

KNOWLEDGE IS MORE THAN FACTS

Knowledge is more than data and information. One of the more significant problems associated with managing and using knowledge is attempting to get to the "truth." Knowledge is an important concept, but for many it remains an ambiguous concept. Many unwittingly include speculation, inference, and rumor under the umbrella of "knowledge." To illustrate the expanse of the "umbrella," look in a thesaurus, or more frequently these days, click on the thesaurus feature of a word processing software package, and words such as *information, facts, data, familiarity, awareness, understanding,* and *comprehension* appear as common appellations. There is a wide gulf between the words' meanings, such as "facts and data," and the words' "understanding and comprehension." Many times people state, "just give me the facts and I'll make the judgment." If one has the right context, critical analytical capacity, and frame of reference, this may be a logical path; however, most people do not possess sufficient backgrounds on complex global subjects to make valid judgments.

An interesting case in point is the study of economic and global perspectives between "expert" and "novice" observers. In reviewing these differences in perspective, Blendon et al. (1997) provide useful insights into the role of knowledge and ability to use knowledge. The researchers used data from the *Washington Post*/Henry J. Kaiser Family Foundation/ Harvard University Survey Project to assess public knowledge on major issues facing the United States. The findings revealed the differences between facts, data, and knowledge. When the general public was asked about their perceptions concerning important issues such as cost of living, job creation, income gaps between rich and poor, as well as perceptions about global economic issues, there was wide divergence between the survey of professional economists and the general public. College graduates tended to hold views closer to the economists than noncollege graduates, but the gulf was still staggering.

A few examples help to highlight these differences. When asked why the economy is not doing better than it is, 77% of the general public thought it was due to the size of the federal deficit; however, only 32% of the economists credited the deficit as the economic nadir. The majority of the general public, 61%, thought high taxes were the reason the economy underperformed as compared with only 18% of the economists. Similarities existed between the general public and the economists on issues of underperformance created though inadequate training and education as well as low levels of personal savings (Blendon et al., 1997).

Economists armed with extensive experience and education on economic matters consistently viewed issues drastically different from the general public. Information and data must be contextualized and blended with ample prior knowledge to be usefully converted into knowledge. The conclusions reached by Blendon et al. (1997) serve as powerful warnings for those engaged in managing knowledge. Individuals may not believe government data or their experiences may not reflect the official data—perceptions and prior experiences create powerful biases.

Media reporting that suffers from "reporting bias" may have significant effects on individuals' perceptions. Americans' economic knowledge foundation is weak, creating difficulties in how Americans assess the performance of the economy.

The research on general public perceptions on specialized topics has interesting implications for knowledge-based leadership. The perception gaps highlight the nature of knowledge, problems of bias, lack of knowledge structures in forming judgments, and the role of expert knowledge. The knowledge "truth" dilemma reminds one of the quaint, poignant, and often repeated stories of the difference between a recession and a depression. If your neighbor is out of work, then the economy is beset by a recession; however, if you are out of work, the economy is in the midst of a depression. It does not matter whether the subject is the economy, technical issues, or a host of other subjects; a lack of expert knowledge creates problems for knowledge leaders. So, how can a leader seek and use relevant knowledge? Leaders must understand the nature of knowledge as well as the environment where knowledge will be employed in order to effectively craft knowledge-based solutions.

THE ECONOMICS OF KNOWLEDGE

We live in a global society where organizations seek to achieve an advantage over rivals. Not-for-profit and governmental agencies seek to distinguish themselves. Unfortunately, as means of knowledge acquisition become ubiquitous and less costly, competitive advantage is temporary, dissipating quickly. What worked yesterday no longer works in today's environment. However, organizations that become skilled at continuous and collaborative learning are proving to be the most adept at defying the economic "law" of diminishing marginal return (Senge, 1990). Knowledge, linked to authority, allows leaders and professionals to rapidly shift and make radical changes to maintain and improve important services at decreasing costs. Seamless and responsive services and products are manifestations of knowledge innovations. Physical and financial assets are important, but knowledge assets and capabilities are now proving to be the key strategic differences among organizations.

Kenneth Boulding (1966) believes knowledge is more critical to economic development than most economists give credit. Boulding states that the role of knowledge is either taken for granted or neglected in three key areas of economic theory: market theory; economic and community development theory; and in the theory of decision making in public and private sectors. It is fair to state that Boulding believes that knowledge is the essential ingredient that explains economic development and social progress. Knowledge creation and social progress flow directly from humans and their unique capabilities. The building blocks of human capabilities are known as human capital.

WHY MANAGE KNOWLEDGE?

History teaches the importance of knowledge. The medieval guild, one of the first forms of incorporation, represents one way of managing knowledge—when knowledge is scarce, hoard it, wrap it in a veil of mystery, and preclude "others" from the inner sanctum. This form of leadership—"knowledge is power"—is still practiced by many organizations today. In this form of organization, knowledge becomes an elixir for maintaining power. Understandably, it represents false power over an organization that is dying a knowledge death. This " knowledge scarcity" or the "I know everything" leader stifles organizational learning. Regretfully, these obsolete forms of leadership are still practiced today in contemporary guilds or the "professions." If we are sick, we see a medical doctor. If we have legal problems, we seek out a licensed attorney. Medical, accounting, and legal knowledge are just a few of the professions where professional knowledge is held tightly within the fences of the guilds—jargon, licensure, and legal restrictions serve as keys to the gates where only a few are allowed to pass. Economists refer to these types of restrictions as "rent-seeking" behavior or behavior that provides extraordinary economic gains based on generalized restrictions to most individuals. At times, there are good reasons to limit practice to those holding specialized knowledge, but in many cases these limitations are taken to extremes, resulting in scarcity of providers. A clear example is the shortage of health care providers in most countries throughout the world—including developed countries. Historical events are replete with examples of knowledge hoarding.

Great battles throughout history have been won or lost on the basis of "intelligence" about the opposing forces. The lack of intelligence results in surprise. Consider the unbelievable feat of Hannibal navigating the mountains on elephants to launch a surprise attack on the Romans about 2,200 years ago. The Romans lacked knowledge of Hannibal's capabilities, resulting in a surprise attack. On December 7, 1941, Pearl Harbor, Hawaii, was attacked and a large portion of the U.S. Pacific Fleet was destroyed. On September 11, 2001, the United States suffered another blistering attack on its native soil when hijacked aircraft careened into the twin World Trade

Towers in New York and the Pentagon in Washington, DC. The after action reviews of both Pearl Harbor and the September 11 attacks highlight that enough information existed to warn of impending doom, but the information was stuck in "silos" and lacked integration to become knowledge that could have prevented the attacks. The vital knowledge that could have warned of the impending attacks was lost in the noise. The knowledge problems faced in the attacks are familiar: too much information and not enough knowledge.

Surprises, due to lack of knowledge about opponents, plague all types of organizations. The steps necessary to prevent surprise and shock are predicated on understanding—understanding the nature and uses of knowledge through a proactive gathering and application of knowledge.

Knowledge is organic in nature. What is meant by organic? Well, it is gathered through all of the senses and integrated in the mind. It is interactive among people. We refine our understanding of a topic as we discuss ideas and concepts with others and consider their perspectives. Knowledge is organic because it is filtered and conditioned by previous experiences and is affected by personal bias (Nosich, 2001). Our understanding of knowledge, or search for truth, is honed through actions and interactions—it is ever changing; it is organic.

Leaders wrestle with the problem of attaining unbiased knowledge and using it effectively. After all, intellectual capital is the sum of the knowledge component of human capital available to the organization. Not only do humans need to acquire and integrate knowledge with prior knowledge; they must also evaluate it critically to reduce bias. Mere acquisition of the knowledge that attacks were pending in 1941 and 2001 would not have been enough to prevent the attacks. The knowledge needed to be integrated, critically evaluated, assessed, and then the implications made known to policy makers. The policy makers would then have been capable of acting upon the knowledge to prevent the attacks.

Data and information are not enough to allow the leader to successfully shape an organization. Knowledge—fully understood—that can be acted upon is the essential element in using knowledge effectively. The leadership challenge is to craft an organizational culture and capability for learning that can meet the mission, respond effectively to change, thrive, and cope well with external challenges.

THREE

THE NATURE OF KNOWLEDGE

No pleasure is comparable to the standing upon the vantage ground of truth . . . and to see the errors and wanderings, and mists, and tempests, in the vale below.

—Francis Bacon, *Francis Bacon, 1551–1626, Of Truth*

Humans are incredible creatures; we pack our heads full of "stuff" and run about repeating variations of what is in our heads. Many hear our utterances and mentally record their version. This chain of transmission typically is not a chain of knowledge; it represents a chained transmission of beliefs and opinions. Beliefs and opinions are assertions that may or may not be truth, and the probability that they are true is less than certain.

What we typically call "knowledge" is really an attempt to present our own version of the truth. Truth is the underlying reality of existence and the state of nature. Absolute knowledge is unwavering certainty and implies that our understanding represents the true state of nature. Accordingly, the information we pack into our heads, and communicate to others, actually represents more of what we believe about knowledge rather than absolute knowledge. Understanding this simple, but often overlooked, truth is essentially the first step in knowledge-based leadership. Leaders who believe they fully comprehend the "truth" are dangerous to themselves and organizations.

Practical leadership requires understanding what an organization "is" and what it "must be" prior to charting a course to new vistas. The wise leader also understands what an organization knows and must know to reach the new vista. The knowledge leadership journey begins with differentiating between knowledge, opinions, and beliefs.

PUTTING THE HORSE BEFORE THE CART

Why study the nature of knowledge? If the notion of knowledge is "fuzzy" then the resultant system will be "fuzzy." In organizations, fuzzy spells trouble. If an organization is going to invest in using knowledge effectively to provide a strategic and operational leadership advantage, then organizational leaders must understand the nature of knowledge. Knowledge management projects were thought to be the zenith of the grand new knowledge-based future promised by management gurus in the 1980s. Unfortunately, the zenith was all too short and did not fulfill its promise. The problems associated with many knowledge management projects coalesce into a few categories:

- developing over ambitious or ambiguous goals
- underestimating the resources required to develop the system
- misunderstanding the nature of knowledge
- developing systems too complex for anyone to use
- deploying technology prior to developing human capital and knowledge system architecture

Every experienced professional, manager, and leader understands that there is always a bit of art in the science of any profession. Mastering the rudiments of the art, philosophy, and science of human learning is a prerequisite to knowledge-based leadership in organizations. A key point worth mentioning is that knowledge-based leadership is knowledge management, and it began with the origin of humans.

NOTIONS OF KNOWLEDGE

Those who seek knowledge must acquire the building blocks such as data and information, but also be able to foster a healthy skepticism about the use of "assumptions" and reliance on facts. Knowledge acquisition and use is a life-long enterprise based on learning, unlearning, and relearning tempered by experience. Organizational knowledge is the sum of an organization's collective learning. Some of the knowledge is tacit—in the heads of the individuals. Some of the knowledge is common, or explicit, and known publicly within an organization. Organizational knowledge is acquired and used in many of the same ways as individual knowledge, but it must be managed differently due to organizational turbulence. Organizational turbulence includes employee turnover, organizational silos that prevent knowledge sharing, and multiple perspectives within an organization.

Since individual human learning is the foundation for organizational learning, it is essential to develop a working understanding of individual learning, thinking, and the role of communication in knowledge generation prior to tackling organizational knowledge development. All that we are or hope to become is related to knowledge. Our framed experiences, values, expert insights, and intuition provide a context for new experience and learning.

The world of knowledge should be viewed as linking individuals to organizations. The following six knowledge abilities link personal growth while enhancing organizational effectiveness (Zwart & Resnick, 2000):

1. gathering knowledge through continuous learning by people within an organization as part of an organized structure
2. organizing knowledge so that it is tied to and integrated with related knowledge
3. distributing knowledge to others so that necessary people can gain quick, and easy, access to knowledge
4. converting knowledge into action to provide increased value goods and services for others
5. training continuously for growth and improvement
6. building a knowledge cycle so that new knowledge and information is continuously added to the learning system, distributed, and applied for solutions of problems

The informed leader understands the link between knowledge and performance and uses that understanding to shape the organization. Understanding the nature, sources, and uses of knowledge are essential leadership responsibilities.

LEVERAGING KNOWLEDGE

The raw power of knowledge to transform an organization is unlimited. Think about the potentials, expanding current knowledge to discover new knowledge and new innovations. Knowledge is the building block in the decision-making and problem-solving processes. Organizations also embed knowledge in their products and services, while using new knowledge to improve products and services. Knowledge touches and shapes all aspects of an organization. Now knowledge is not the only ingredient in human success—other attributes that compose human capital also contribute—but knowledge is an essential ingredient in leveraging humans to foster success in an organization.

New medical procedures that extend and improve the quality of life are built upon the grist of facilitating knowledge growth and transfer. Developing new strategies to solve the complex problems facing our globalized societies are knowledge-based propositions. Only through the formal development and application of knowledge can institutions and organizations create value. Value that enriches humans is the only reason organizations exist. For the leader, understanding knowledge-based solutions begins with a review of the fundamental concepts associated with human learning.

FUNDAMENTALS OF HUMAN LEARNING

Cognitive psychologists have spent a great deal of time studying the process of learning and have written many books on the topic. Yet, the concept of knowledge remains elusive to many of us—even though it may not appear to be elusive. Thankfully, there are certain concepts of human learning that can be drawn upon to frame the fundamentals of knowledge acquisition. Most people are familiar with the basics of constructing a building. The building process provides a good framework to describe the process of learning.

A general contractor is selected to integrate the necessary tasks to complete a building project. They select a good "building" team and coordinate the activities of the team. To start the process, an architect drafts a complete set of drawings prior to beginning a construction project. Teams of engineers calculate load and stress limits to determine appropriate material usage and construction techniques. When the day arrives to begin construction, the foundation is laid and a framing structure is built upon the foundation. Beam by beam support structures are connected, initially surrounded by scaffolding to provide support. Subsequent layers of finishing materials are added to complete the construction process. After construction, and the passage of time, renovations are required to update the building's usefulness.

Learning is like the construction process. Leaders are the general contractors, providing guidance and coordinating the learning activities of an organization. Planning activities that frame learning and knowledge use are akin to the architectural drawings that guide an organization. Then knowledge foundations are laid—declarative knowledge consisting of "organized data and facts." Framing knowledge, such as procedural knowledge, that connects skills and performance to facts and data is added to the knowledge capabilities of individuals and hence the organization. Framing knowledge represents the "how to do" component of knowledge (Derry, 1990). The primary knowledge structure is complete when we add the finishing touches—conditional knowledge that lets people know when and why to apply knowledge (Simon, 1980). Knowledge employed with proper planning and coordination creates an environment for success; however, knowledge employed under vague conditions can lead to disaster.

John Dewey (1910), the great American educator and philosopher, provided additional insight into the nature of knowledge by differentiating between thought and thinking. Dewey referred to thought as anything that enters the head—the "stuff." Thinking is the engaging of thoughts by connecting and reflecting on them. In essence, thinking is attempting to assess thoughts as probable or improbable beliefs and potentially validate them as truth. Dewey believed that there should be training in the process of thinking. In today's language, Dewey was putting forth a philosophy for thinking that includes knowledge acquisition, decision making, creative and critical thinking skills, reflection, and problem solving.

BUILDING KNOWLEDGE BLOCKS

Building and using individual and organizational knowledge are creative processes. An author uses mental imagery loaded with meaning to guide writing. The intended meaning is laid down in writing on the pages by the author. After the author writes, the control of the meaning is lost. Every reader that picks up the author's material comes away with his or her own learned meaning and interpretation of the author. And so it is with all forms of beliefs and opinions that are sorted through human intellectual filters as the ideas are being shaped to find true knowledge.

At this point, it is extremely important to point out a commonly held fallacy about knowledge that plagues knowledge strategies in many organizations. The author example provides a good vehicle to illustrate "knowledge plague." The author has knowledge, and through mediation—reading the book—the reader creates knowledge, which is typically not exactly the same as the meaning intended by the author. Since the reader and the author do not have the exact same set of experiences, education, and perspectives, the environment for knowledge construction is not the same—and cannot be exactly the same. A book is merely a mediation device to communicate the author's knowledge. A book does not contain knowledge. It conveys information, data, and messages, but the reader constructs knowledge from the information, data, and messages. Books are inanimate; only humans create knowledge. Here is the punch line: humans create and communicate with other humans who create knowledge—the device to mediate the communication does not contain knowledge. Potential knowledge can be embedded in the mediation devices, but not "knowledge"—that is the domain of humans.

The notions of knowledge acquisition and shared use is not as fuzzy or hopeless as it may first seem, but it is important to gain a firm understanding of the "softness" of knowledge and the mechanisms to construct knowledge. To manage knowledge, or truth, one must have a firm grasp on the essential nature of knowledge. As the old saying goes, one cannot manage what one does not understand. Theories of learning fall into three broad categories: cultural transmission and language transmission (Vygotsky, 1962), strategic learning, and the developmental school (McKeough, 1991).

In the cultural transmission model, language and shared symbols are viewed as the essential way of representing objects, events, and concepts that lack physical presence. Humans are arguably unique in their ability to use complex language in infinite combinations to construct meaning. Learners internalize complex events and ideas through language and develop mental, or cognitive, scaffolds to structure the learned events. Scaffolds are constantly being torn down and rebuilt with new learning acquisition and elaboration.

Elaboration is simply the linking of one knowledge point to another to build new knowledge relationships. For instance, if I am told that when the wind blows, loose items blow around, I create a link between blowing wind and items blowing around. If later I am told that the wind makes the temperature feel lower than the temperature displayed by the thermometer, I build another knowledge link about wind. By thoughtful reflection and more observation, I make the connection that when I see leaves blow, I expect my skin to feel cooler than the temperature readings. This process of observation linking and cognitive expansion is known as elaboration.

The strategic learning theory suggests that developmental levels may limit or enhance learning capacities. This theory views learning as "information processing." Information processing development is best illustrated through the context of the differences between novice and experts. Experts know how to best solve problems in their expert fields. This is due to the amount of knowledge they possess and their ability to regulate knowledge and make combinations that novices are not capable of doing. Researchers are beginning to speculate that intuition is really expert knowledge applied at fast cognitive speeds (King & Appleton, 1997).

The three basic learning models taken together provide keen insights into the learning process (McKeough, 1991). They suggest that knowledge is acquired through the language process, construction of knowledge, and through intellectual information processing. Learning theory is interesting, but how can leaders use these theories to improve organizational performance? Leaders need to understand that learning is different for everyone, and each theory provides a useful piece to the knowledge puzzle. Leaders should foster self-regulated learning (metacognition) in an organization—this is a skill that experts possess. For instance, expert readers draw on many cues while reading, including strong metacognitive skills. If knowledge leaders are responsible for mentoring employees to become self-actuated learners, then they must fully understand metacognitive skills.

METACOGNITION AS A LEARNING STRATEGY

The quick definition for metacognition is one that includes notions of self-awareness, instinctive reflection, and control of one's thinking (Houston, 1995). Paris, Cross, and Lipson (1984) describe self-governed learning by concluding that thinkers need to possess declarative knowledge (facts, details, and the ability to describe thinking strategies), procedural knowledge (how to use the selected strategy), and conditional knowledge (when to use fact, details, and thinking strategies). Swartz and Perkins (1989) distinguish four levels of thought that are increasingly metacognitive:

1. Tacit Use: Internalized individual thinking—decision making—typically without consciously thinking about it (automaticity).
2. Aware Use: Aware of conscious thought.
3. Strategic Use: Organizes thinking by way of particular conscious strategies that enhance learning efficacy.
4. Reflective Use: Reflects upon thinking before and after or even in the middle of the thinking process, while considering how to proceed and how to improve.

Metacognition is the self-regulation of the learning process or the ability to relate content, context, and prior knowledge with new knowledge gained in the learning process. Over time humans develop automaticity where advanced learning skills are employed automatically without conscious effort. Automaticity can be better understood by comparing it to riding a bicycle.

When one first starts riding a bicycle, it takes extreme concentration on motor skills, balance, and awareness of obstacles. Over time, the process becomes automatic and the rider can contemplate other issues or just enjoy the ride without focusing on "riding" the bike. Automaticity allows individuals to regulate common activities, while attending to other activities.

So what does the development of metacognitive capabilities mean to the professional or a leader? A great deal! Any attempt to develop a learning and knowledge rich organization without developing advanced learners within the organization is doomed to failure. Learning models and metacognition are the building blocks of crafting an environment for learning. A word of caution—learning and unlearning are ongoing processes. It is important to understand that the knowledge acquisition and application process is iterative, fragmented, and biased. Human knowledge is limited by the finiteness of human perceptive capabilities. Organizations that lack a disciplined approach to the use of knowledge could appropriately call their knowledge-based system a belief-based system.

HUMAN KNOWLEDGE CREATION

Lessons from knowledge creation in science provide deep and profound insights into how humans develop and use knowledge. The role of perception in learning is critical in understanding the limitations of human knowledge. Jacob Bronowski (1978), a noted 20th-century scientist, wrote and spoke about the role of biology in filtering human understanding of reality, as well the "masons" approach to knowledge that humans must endure due to our limited faculties. The masons approach—my choice of terms not Bronowski's choice—suggests that knowledge is built brick by brick and until the brick structure is complete, its true identity cannot be revealed.

This painstaking "brick-by-brick" knowledge-building process limits human understanding of reality. What we think of as true today, we find false tomorrow and jettison old notions of reality. Newtonian physics was once viewed as truth, but it gave way to newer views of physics by Einstein and others. Our understanding of social phenomenon is constantly being expanded. One major complication is that knowledge, unlike the wall, does not usually have a blueprint, so we build false portions of the wall that must be later broken down and replaced.

To further complicate the concept of knowledge discovery, Bronowski suggests that what we see with our eyes is not reality, but a chemical process that is enhanced by the biological functions of our mind. We see grainy images, but our mind is programmed to refine the images based on human biology and experience. We see our "minds" version of reality— other animals see reality differently. Our visual perception of the world is a powerful ingredient in the knowledge acquisition process, but the way we communicate our perceptions helps us to refine and ultimately transmit knowledge. Our communicative capabilities, according to Bronowski, are symbolic in nature. Word and sentence structures are innovative and complex, allowing infinite combinations of meanings.

Meanings must be processed according to a vast array of individual experiences. It is this vastness of perception, interpretation, and meaning creation that makes knowledge unique for almost all individuals. Who among us has experienced all of the same experiences? We do have common experiences, but our experiences are each unique in adding to our understanding of events. If there were 6 billion people on Earth, then there would be 6 billion philosophies of life.

Organizational leaders must develop a full appreciation for the role and uniqueness of knowledge before they can use it to align an organization and create value. Our understanding of the world—what we typically call knowledge—is literally created by each individual. However, we must move from concepts about knowledge to pragmatic categorization of knowledge to harness its power. The concept of professional intellect is that tool.

FOUR

WINNING WITH PROFESSIONAL INTELLECT

Success is that old ABC—ability, breaks, and courage.

—Charles Luckman, *World of Quotes.com*

The key task leaders get paid to do is make quality decisions that lead to value creation. There are many desired qualities that good leaders should possess, but the ability to establish focused goals and objectives and to make quality decisions to achieve those goals is paramount. To accomplish these paramount leadership tasks, effective leaders must be capable of

- selecting the "right" people for organizational needs
- developing people
- organizing people for knowledge-based problem solving
- transcending resource limitations by empowering people to innovate

In today's hypercompetitive world that thrives on knowledge, leaders must tap individual knowledge and channel it to enhance decision making. This means the leader must be driven to achieve results, not satisfy personal ego needs. Since goals frame results and results are achieved through people, then people are of foremost importance for the leader. Leaders must be capable of balancing skills, talents, knowledge, and interpersonal needs of people in achieving organization goals (Robbins & Finley, 2000). This balancing act typically takes place in teams. Teams fall into two basic categories: project teams and functional, or organizational, teams (Robbins & Finley, 2000). Project teams are formed to achieve a specific goal and then disband. Functional, or organizational, teams are permanent and are typically known as work groups or departments. Functional teams have, by their very nature, constantly evolving goals. Knowledge-based problem solutions are typically resolved in teams. Accordingly, leaders must be skilled in organizing, selecting, mentoring, and establishing goals for teams. Robbins and Finley (2000) suggest that knowledge workers succeed best in environments that have a degree of hierarchy. Goal establishment, as well as who is responsible for what and when, is a key ingredient in establishing team hierarchy and empowering teams. When team members know the "who, what, where, and when," they are empowered to focus on meeting team goals, and avoid becoming enmeshed in team politics. With structure determined, the next step entails blending the right mixture of people into teams—knowledge resides in teams. Leaders should

- Establish goals and objectives that enable success.
- Establish time limits to meet goals. If team goals extend beyond 60 days, build in subordinate goals that build toward ultimate goal accomplishment that can be met within 60 days.
- Build team membership structured for success.
- Link team knowledge and capabilities to goals and objectives to enable quality leadership decision making.

PROFESSIONAL INTELLECT

Identification of the right people to hire, develop, and commit to teams is one of the most vexing problems a leader faces. One of the more practical frameworks for solving the hiring, development, and selection problem lies in the concept of the professional intellect. J. B. Quinn, Anderson, and Finkelstein (1996) posit that professionals command a body of knowledge that should evolve through levels. They suggest that the professional intellect embodying this knowledge operates at four levels:

- Cognitive or "know-what" knowledge is gained through study and certification. This level is typically considered declarative knowledge.
- Advanced "know-how" skills are gained through experience and knowledge elaboration. Attainment of this level of professional intellect enhances the ability to solve application type problems many times by using professional best practices. This level of knowledge capability can be thought of as procedural knowledge.
- System understanding or "know-why" knowledge is grounded in deep critical thinking capabilities. At this level, the individual understands "cause and effect relationships underlying a profession." This level is the embodiment of conditional knowledge and reflects the capacity for high levels of abstract, critical, and reflective reasoning.
- Self-motivated creativity or "care-why" is the psychological backbone that encourages employees to use knowledge effectively through developed positive professional behaviors for success. (p. 72)

Professional intellect is a powerful concept that allows leaders to link knowledge capabilities with organizational outcomes. Armed with an understanding of these knowledge levels, leaders can hire, develop, and select individuals for teams that embody the right mix of knowledge for success.

CRITICAL THINKING

Critical, creative, and reflective thinking skills are essential in achieving a "know-why" level of professional knowledge. Critical and creative thinking can be viewed in broad terms as thinking with purpose, clarity, and with interpretive intent. At times, people claim, "You must maintain an open-mind with respect to ideas." What one should say is that "a critical mind maintains receptiveness to ideas but makes informed judgments about the idea after careful reflection."

Taken to the extreme, a completely open mind is a vacuous mind where judgments are never made. Leaders must make judgments to make decisions. Our whole frame of reference of reality and truth as well as our ability to "get things done" are based on the ability to make judgments. Thinking critically to make judgments is a discipline—the scientific method of inquiry is built on critical thinking. Leading experts in critical thinking, Richard Paul and Linda Elder (2004), from the Foundation for Critical Thinking, suggest the following elements in framing analytical, or critical, thought:

1. Consider the purpose, goal, or objective of thinking.
2. Address the question at issue.
3. Consider data, facts, observations, and experiences that frame the information to be evaluated.
4. Make explicit interpretation and inferences of implied solutions and conclusions.
5. Analyze concepts through consideration of the theories, definitions, axioms, laws, principles, and models applied to the information.
6. Analyze the assumptions, presuppositions, and items taken for granted.
7. Articulate implications and consequences.
8. Consider multiple points of view, frames of reference, perspectives, and orientations.

Wise leaders will apply Paul and Elder's elements of critical thought in decision making. Leaders should also establish a climate for decision making that embraces professional intellect. Specifically, leaders must craft an environment that is trusting, that is open to ideas, and that suspends final judgment until all facts are presented. In addition to thinking skills, listening skills are equally essential to leaders and team members during their decision-making processes. Critical listening is intimately linked to the critical-thinking process and focuses on an attempting to "hear" and understand the speaker's perspective in order to improve one's own understanding (Chaffee, 2002).

Practicing "knowledge use" can initially be painful for an organization. Efficiency of decision making may initially be slower; however, the benefits of knowledge use far outweigh any temporary discomfort. In time, decision making will become faster and better using knowledge-based leadership methods. Just like the would-be athlete training previously underused muscles and suffering through the resulting soreness, organizations must exercise knowledge use "muscles." There is a discipline in using creative and critical thought to foster knowledge development in an organization that must be inculcated and practiced. Thinking, knowledge use, and understanding cannot be delegated to computers, systems, or other forms of technology. The essential elements in leading a knowledgeable organization are singularly human. There is no "short-cut" technological fix for knowledge leadership.

MOTIVATION FOR LEARNING

Why do people choose to learn? What do people do with the knowledge? How can learning and knowledge be harnessed for organizational success? We find the answers to these questions in the field of psychology. One of the more practical theories about learning that has gained respect in the fields of education, business, and psychology is social learning theory. The theory emphasizes the role of learning through observation and modeling (e.g., vicarious learning). The theory also explores the influence of individual thinking on motivation, effectiveness of learning, and the ability to do something with knowledge after learning (Bandura, 1977). Basically, the theory posits that learners make determinations about self-efficacy and expected outcomes. If learners believe they can master the knowledge and have positive expectations about the result of the learning, then they are motivated to learn.

Research confirms the usefulness of Bandura's theory in understanding the role of learning and knowledge in an organization. Literally, the theory underscores the importance of experience, environment, and cooperative learning in an organization. Organizations that merely attempt to package knowledge in a "technology" solution or through other forms of mediated communication will be disappointed with their learning and knowledge-based efforts.

The implications are plain: Individuals learn by doing, observing, and refining their knowledge. Since many individuals are not confident in their learning abilities, leaders must be proficient in knowledge "pointing," mentoring, and coaching. Research also suggests that there is a link between knowledge leadership styles and motivation. An emphasis on open one-to-one communication can produce shifts in professional behavior, motivation, and learning. According to social learning theory, leadership style establishes the organizational learning environment (Harrison & McIntosh, 1992).

Research further suggests that behavior modeling is an important component in leadership. Knowledge, skills, and behaviors, all foundations of human capital, are essentially cued and transmitted through observation and modeling (Decker, 1986). Decker provides a useful checklist to assist in building a motivated learning organization:

1. Identify the knowledge, skills, and behaviors that lead to improved organizational performance.
2. Select the models, such as live demonstrations, collaborative work, or other models of knowledge sharing, that are most appropriate for the organization.
3. Select individuals for knowledge acquisition that can benefit the organization through the acquisition of the identified knowledge, skills, and abilities.
4. Structure an environment to maximize attention and reproduction of the modeled knowledge.
5. Reinforce and model the targeted knowledge, skills, and behaviors. Clearly demonstrate the positive consequences of engaging in using knowledge, skills, and behaviors that benefit the organization.
6. Provide individuals with tools for mental rehearsal, such as online tools, written material, and access to colleagues, that possess the target knowledge, skills, and abilities.
7. Allow individuals to practice the new knowledge, skills, and behaviors in multiple situations and through multiple simulations
8. Provide honest, but nonthreatening, feedback.
9. Continue building upon the new foundation knowledge, skills, and behaviors.

Organizing an approach to knowledge building is straightforward: The knowledge, skills, and behaviors important to an organization are identified, linked to organizational success, transferred, evaluated, and reinforced. Random communication of fleeting portions of knowledge will not have long-term effects in an organization. There is no silver bullet or magic elixir to transfer knowledge. It takes leadership, planning, hard work, and consistency to build a learning organization. Popular culture has shaped people to expect immediate gratification and instant results

(Lasch, 1979). Building human capital takes time and patience. The investment in a knowledge approach to organizational success is tied to the resource-intensive business of building human capital. Smart leaders resist "popular culture" quick-fix temptations.

MULTIPLE PERSPECTIVES

While the principles of learning and thinking are universal, perspectives about knowledge and truth are not. All of us suffer from limited perspectives—we are human. But how can knowledge-based organizations, some with multiple locations across many continents, manage multiple perspectives? First, recognize that there are multiple perspectives and these perspectives shade views of common events. Second, expose employees to multiple perspectives to improve their ability to understand differing views. Third, help those within the organization to understand the "soft" nature of knowledge. Last, evaluate knowledge within an organization to validate its accuracy or usefulness for organizational success.

Vincent Ryan Ruggiero (1998) provides useful insight for assisting individuals in gaining an awareness of their own and differing perspectives. Ruggiero suggests that individuals need to be assisted in becoming "self-aware, self-critical, and self-enhancing" (p. 13). He believes that individuals must be capable of looking at themselves "honestly and objectively" in order to appreciate multiple perspectives (p. 43). Further, Ruggiero notes that in order to evolve a sense of multiple perspectives, the individual must not allow the senses to control thinking but be systematically controlled by thinking. The senses can be overwhelmed by impressions shaped by an individual's perspective. Ruggiero suggests three basic steps in achieving independence as an individual and crafting the ability to view multiple perspectives appropriately:

1. "Acknowledge the influences that shape your thinking."
2. "Sort out and evaluate your ideas and attitudes."
3. Choose the best ideas by resisting the pressures of habit and resistance to change. (pp. 44–45)

Leaders recognize the role of perspective in knowledge use.

DEVELOPING ORGANIZATIONAL THINKING

What does all of this nature of knowledge mean? One must be aware of the fundamentals of how humans learn, the nature of knowledge, and the implications of using knowledge to help build successful organizations. Jeanne Ellis Ormrod (1999) pulls together some important generalizations about the nature of knowledge. Ormrod notes that humans store information in multiple ways to facilitate recall and elaboration. Additionally, knowledge is generalized rather than event specific. People use concepts to summarize events, and these generalizations form the backbone of learning. Generalized learning has several advantages (Ormrod):

- Reduces the complexity of the world to manageable notions
- Allows knowledge application in new situations
- Facilitates abstraction
- Enhances the efficacy of thought
- Enhances connections among the things we know to things we do not know

Ormrod observes that integrated knowledge is more important than fragmented knowledge. Embedding important pieces of information that we know in the learning process enhances the ability to draw inferences. An in-depth knowledge of a few topics is more beneficial to individual performance than a superficial understanding on many different topics.

PROPOSITIONAL VERSUS PRESCRIPTIVE KNOWLEDGE

Economic historian Joel Moykr (2002) provides an interesting glimpse into the role of knowledge in shaping economic history. Moykr borrows the definitions of useful knowledge (Kuznets, 1965) to frame his debate between propositional and prescriptive knowledge. The cousins of these two categorizations of knowledge are descriptive, procedural, and conditional knowledge. Moykr's angle is useful in defining not only the nature of knowledge, but it is useful for leaders—it helps them understand what to know and when to know it.

Propositional knowledge is the science or art in the field of endeavor. For instance, in organizations it can be the body of knowledge associated with the science underlying the product or the knowledge of human nature if the organization is in a service field. Alternately, prescriptive knowledge is the "how to" or "when to" aspect of knowledge. The use of this knowledge is best defined as a technique within propositional knowledge. Given the current state of propositional knowledge, there can be many forms of prescriptive knowledge (techniques) employed to solve a problem (Scheffler, 1965). Leaders build the right mix of knowledge and human capital capabilities in an organization to improve the organization's probability for success. Some leaders become mesmerized by one type of knowledge or the other and load teams full of people who possess a specific knowledge. This approach can only lead to disaster. The insightful leader balances teams with individuals who possess different knowledge, skills, talents, and behaviors. Team diversification goes beyond gender, race, and the like—it also includes knowledge, perspectives, and orientations.

CRAFTING KNOWLEDGE SOLUTIONS

At one end of the leadership spectrum, leaders believe in complete group decision making, which can result in groupthink. Groupthink suffers from a lack of accountability for the decisions made and often results in less than optimum decisions since groups attempt to find consensus—they achieve the lowest common denominator. At the other end of the spectrum, the "fearless" leader attempts to make all of the decisions. This person is doomed to failure or just succeeds through blind luck.

Good knowledge-based judgments and decisions are hybrid decisions. Leadership is an "active" endeavor. Leaders make judgments, decisions, and exercise control but should be informed by team members who have the requisite knowledge to assist the leader. Leaders with an excessive need for control must learn to jettison this "need." Knowledge leadership is about attaining results (guiding not directing), and the degree of control exerted by leaders is tied to how best to achieve results. Excessive control shuts down necessary participation by others in knowledge-rich environments. Remember, individuals own their knowledge and sound leadership encourages the full sharing of knowledge. Teams should be structured and empowered in a manner that encourages sharing of knowledge. Shared knowledge improves decision making and ultimately improves organizational alignment and control. Leaders build knowledge teams and are willing to share elements of the decision-making process and control with the team in return for improved performance. Leaders cannot share responsibility for the decisions, but smart leaders use teams to flush out the issues, build knowledge, provide context, broaden perspectives, and gain acceptance.

KNOWLEDGE SUPPORT SYSTEMS

Building and sustaining knowledge in an organization is time-consuming but purposeful. Leaders must be capable of answering the following key questions and providing appropriate guidance for the teams in order to gain meaningful results:

- What is the nature of the team?
- Why is this team being formed?
- What is team's mission?
- What resources may be required to successfully implement strategies devised by knowledge teams?
- What are the current resources available to implement team recommendations/solutions?
- Who is responsible for assembling and developing knowledge assets within the team?
- What is the time limit for a decision and how long can the team take to develop the appropriate research and knowledge?

Technology and communication are enhancers and critical linkages to knowledge building, but they are not knowledge. They are precursors to knowledge. At times, leaders quip, "Our people are our primary resource" shortly before they make people redundant and build a new facility or implement a new technology only to find out that the new technology did not solve the underlying problems. Knowledge building is a long-run proposition for success and people are the backbone to this important enterprise.

LEADERSHIP, RISK, AND MANAGING KNOWLEDGE

According to Webster, knowledge is a "clear perception of truth" (Langenscheidt's Pocket Dictionary, 1999, p. 415). Another definition suggests that knowledge is "something learned and kept in the mind" (p. 415). These two definitions provide a solid platform to frame the roles knowledge plays in changing social views. As knowledge was discovered and shared over the past millennia, the worldview of truth—knowledge—also changed. Over the past 50 years, a view formed among some to suggest there is no objective truth or knowledge. They suggest that all knowledge is subjective based on culture, values, and other influences. The term that best captures this sentiment, or philosophy, is *postmodernism*. An extreme version of postmodernism is nihilism, implying that traditional views and values are ungrounded, leading to the notion that life is relatively useless. The problem with these subjective and blurry guideposts is that without ultimate truth, there can be no ultimate knowledge—everything is subjective. Leaders that must produce tangible results cannot succeed in subjective cultures. Unfortunately, popular Western cultures that influence employees contain subjective elements.

Leaders need pragmatic and objective views of an issue. Karl Popper (1979) provides a competing view of subjective truth, one that is useful for leaders. Popper suggests that the primary goal of science and philosophy should be the search for truth. Popper believes that clear and careful statements can be built as theories and models and tested for "truth." The objective model is an essential baseline for leaders seeking usable knowledge. Popper rejects subjectivism arguing, by which "standard" should one judge subjective truth if not by an objective standard? He concludes by stating, "If this form of subjective instrumentalism is true, then it leads to its own refutation. Therefore it cannot be true" (pp. 64–65). Can these two worldviews of knowledge be reconciled to allow practical evaluation and management of knowledge?

Yes, these two views can be reconciled. To design and implement a systems approach to knowledge—not just an information systems approach—use a simple objective model for creating value through knowledge that includes the following elements:

1. Understand that knowledge is expansive, but to be useful to an organization it must be linked to organizational "needs."
2. Assess the current stock of knowledge available against future needs and determine "knowledge gaps."
3. Create a system of knowledge acquisition and management.
4. Apply new knowledge to attain the desired future state.
5. Reject the notion that "everything is relative."
6. Validate the usefulness of knowledge in creating value for organizational stakeholders.
7. Integrate "new knowledge" in the decision-making process.

Boulding (1966) was prophetic in stating, "We have a certain . . . paradox, that where knowledge is an essential part of the system, knowledge about the system changes the system itself" (p. 7). Boulding is not suggesting that knowledge cannot be managed or acquired, only that it is dynamic and the use of knowledge in an organization not only needs management, but requires visionary leadership as well.

BRIEF HISTORY OF KNOWLEDGE MANAGEMENT

Knowledge leadership and management are not necessarily the same thing; however, maintaining a leadership bias in the management process is essential. Gary Yukl (2002), a leading expert on leadership, provides insight into the differences between leading and managing. Yukl notes that the nature of managerial efforts includes supervising, planning and organizing, making decisions, monitoring, controlling, and communicating. Yukl points out that leader tasks permeate all managing tasks and also include task-oriented, relationship-oriented, and participative behaviors. Participative behaviors can be transformative in nature. Managers do things right, but leaders do the right thing.

Using knowledge to add value in organizations grew from the thinking of Peter Drucker in the 1970s and the writings of Ikujiro Nonaka, David Garvin, and many others during the 1980s and 1990s. The organizational knowledge applications have typically emanated from the information technology field. However, a clever researcher can track the notions of knowledge management back to Adam Smith in the 18th-century Enlightenment period, Martin Luther in the 15th and 16th centuries, and still further back to the ancients such as Aristotle's writings on reason and knowledge.

Knowledge transfers—early forms of knowledge management—are linked to early migrations that transferred knowledge from one locality to another. Ancient dialogues and analects collected and allowed for the transfer of knowledge. Knowledge transfer and management are not new, but they are increasingly important in our daily lives. One may correctly state that we are moving from the practice of knowledge management to the art and science of knowledge leadership—the discovery and application of new knowledge through planned activities to achieve organizational success.

Knowledge leadership is a multifaceted activity that consists of insights and abilities for managing and leading organizations. It does not matter whether the aspiring knowledge leader is engaged in a for-profit business, a not-for-profit organization, a governmental organization, or an educational institution because the principles of knowledge are universal and apply equally to all forms of organizations.

To use knowledge as a key component in achieving strategic and operational success, one must not only employ the "tools" of the trade, but must also have a fundamental understanding of the nature of knowledge as it flows through people in an organization. Knowledge is critical to our daily lives and must be guided in a systemic fashion to provide a full range of benefits.

FIVE

HUMAN CAPITAL: CONNECTING KNOWLEDGE TO HUMAN PERFORMANCE

Those who believe in our ability do more than stimulate us. They create for us an atmosphere in which it becomes easier to succeed.

—John Lancaster Spalding, "Aphorisms and Reflections: Conduct, Culture, and Religion," *Webster's Treasury of Relevant Questions*

Human capital—the term carries a capitalistic flair. Calling human capabilities "capital" implies employees are equivalent to other forms of capital. Nothing could be further from the truth; human capital is the antecedent for all forms of capital. Human capital, in the most simple of terms, is the accumulated capacity of an individual. It is the essence of an individual that generates innovation, productivity, and creativity.

Some of the key characteristics, or variables, of human capital include physical skills, perception skills, thinking or cognitive skills, effective communication, generalized and specialized experience, knowledge, cultural and social skills, as well as behavioral habits. These levels of human capital define the potential of humans to perform.

The conversion of knowledge, skills, and talents to performance is the critical link in the chain of knowledge value in an organization. The notion of human performance capacity is as old as recorded history, but the term *human capital* has only been around since the middle of the 20th century.

The organizational stakes associated with understanding and developing human capital are huge. Not only must leaders understand human capital, but leaders must also possess the ability to effectively deploy, link, and nurture it as one of the organization's most precious forms of capital. Recent studies and writings concerning the value of human capital highlight its importance in achieving organizational goals (Amernic, 2003; Pfau & Kay, 2002). The bottom line "secret" to effectively employing human capital is basic: Know what the organization stands for, hire right, employ it properly, and develop it aggressively. As a leader, focus your energy on getting the human capital equation right and most of the other organizational tasks will become much easier.

HOW HUMAN CAPITAL AFFECTS ORGANIZATIONS

A recent study by Watson Wyatt Worldwide (Pfau & Kay, 2002) connects human capital management practices to shareholder value. The conclusions, while derived from studies of for-profit businesses, apply equally to all types of organizations. Human capital accounts for at least 30% of the value generated by businesses. Insightful leadership can increase human potential infinitely, and the leadership techniques are not rocket science. Why do people work, move up the organizational ladder, take risks, and perform at high levels? They react to financial and psychic incentives.

The keys to unlocking the value treasure chest in an organization through human capital lies in providing incentives that matter to employees, such as

- establishing and communicating goals,
- establishing expectations,
- establishing a "productive" cultural environment that emphasizes trust, and
- evaluating employee effectiveness and development opportunities.

A surprising finding uncovered in the Watson Wyatt study concerns the quality recruitment of human capital. Specifically, understanding organizational human capital needs and hiring "right" for these needs have the most significant impact on an organization. Training and development— long considered the most important elements—yield the lowest return. In fact, training employees for their next position, and not focusing on the current position, actually nets a 2% decline in shareholder value.

Some researchers go so far as to state that hiring the right person to spur growth in an organization is paramount in attaining success (Schuster & Zingheim, 1992). Unfortunately, pay and reward (incentive) systems in many cases do not link employee recruitment, retention, and performance to organizational performance. Often, organizations spend a great effort focusing on internal factors such as internal equity rather than focusing on building human capital policies—including pay systems—that create appropriate incentives for employees. Linking pay, rewards, and benefits to organizational goals is the most efficacious method to achieve high-quality human capital performance. Excellent knowledge leaders reject bureaucratic policies and recognize that knowledge-based organizations flourish when the right human capital is aligned though incentives to achieve organization goals.

Leaders always knew that people were important. Now research can begin to quantify just how important they are. Amernic (2003) notes that old rules of thumb in business suggest that 30% of returns are due to physical capital—having the right plant, equipment, and tools available for employees to do their work. We now know that raw human capital capability is at least as important as physical capital in the returns of a business.

The big lesson for organizations is hire right for the position, manage human capital with an eye to achieving organizational goals, tie incentives to performance, and establish a positive climate for performance. A great number of misconceptions about human capital exist, some generated out of bias and ignorance, others by reliance on early human capital studies. The knowledge-based leader achieves results through human capital and must fully appreciate the most recent advances in understanding this all-important form of capital.

EARLY BELIEFS ABOUT HUMAN CAPITAL

A Nobel Prize–winning economist, Theodore Schultz, coined the term *human capital*. Schultz (1961) initially used the appellation of human capital to describe the financial returns associated with investments in developing human capability. The early investigators of human capital focused largely on economic benefits associated with on-the-job training, formal education, and generalized experience (Becker, 1964; E. F. Denison, 1962; Mincer, 1958; Schultz, 1961). A heralded economic scholar, George Psacharopoulos (1973), convincingly argues that early observers of economic phenomenon, such as Adam Smith in the 18th century, fully realized the relationship between economic growth and education.

Yet the powerful impact of human capability in organizational growth laid in wait until economists in the 1950s began to notice that total economic output grew faster than the added "physical" inputs such as labor hours, materials, and so forth. This excess of output over input is known as the residual. The residual was attributed to technical changes or shifts. Study of this residual phenomenon led to increased attention to the quality of labor and began the study of human capital.

Economists wanted to better understand how human capital was formed and shaped to increase productivity. They believed by understanding the nature of human capital, they could prescribe methods to increase productivity. What they found is that human capital transformed value creation. The early empirical investigations into human capital paired human capital with productivity and education (E. F. Denison, 1967) as well as education and wage growth (Schultz, 1961). The early attempts at assessing the role of formal education in developing human capital were known as alpha studies (Psacharopoulos, 1975). The alpha studies placed the role of formal education in explaining "growth" at between 65 and 100%. These studies differentiated between primary, secondary, and higher education, but the results were inconsistent.

Subsequent research, building upon the alpha studies, showed a degree of deep understanding and subtlety about just how humans shaped productivity. Interestingly, one study noted that in developing countries the highest returns to education were garnered by primary levels of education that developed basic literacy and numeracy (Boissiere, Knight, & Sabot, 1985). Other studies linked the benefits of education to other elements of the human capital productivity chain such as the role of literacy in extending life expectancy (Cochrane, 1980). Some researchers noted the genetic link between ability and performance—talent (Griliches & Mason, 1972). From the inception of the term *human capital* in the 1950s, economists added new explanations for economic developments associated with humans. The economists developed the role of human capital to include the dimensions of skill, ability, talent, and then behaviors. In the 1980s and beyond, the study of human capital became a cross-discipline study. Management gurus, psychologists, sociologists, biologists, and medical researchers all began exploring the nature and roles of human capital.

HUMAN CAPITAL COMES OF AGE

Management researchers sought to make employing human capital heuristic by replacing the "where there is smoke there is fire" empiricism of the economists with a practical instrument for improving human performance. They refined common characteristics of human capital to include pragmatic definitions of knowledge, skills, abilities, behavior, culture, and performance motivation. Several researchers developed fully integrated models of human capital and organization performance that include the role of motivation and performance incentives (Dretske, 1988; Schuster & Zingheim, 1992; Tobin, 1998). Some writers, researchers, and practitioners do not even use the term *human capital*. They describe and analyze elements of human capital without directly referring to the nomenclature of human capital.

THE INVESTOR MODEL OF HUMAN CAPITAL

Thomas Davenport (1999) takes an integrated approach to human capital, suggesting that the basic building blocks include a cognitive component (knowledge), a competency component (skill), genetic aptitude (talent), and a performance component (behavior). Taken together these components form human capital ability and are additive. According to Davenport, there are human capital multipliers such as time and effort. Many definitions of the foundation components of human capital parallel Davenport's model, but Davenport takes a unique behavioral twist that adds robustness and practicality to the human capital model.

Davenport suggests that individuals invest in building human capital, but they are also investors in applying their human capital. People have a stock of human capital, but what does it take to get them to "invest" their human capital into the organization? By considering the employee-investor model of human capital, leaders gain insights into the role of the individual in organizational success.

Individuals are "in the drivers seat" in the human capital–investor model. They decide how much knowledge and other forms of ability they will garner and apply in helping to build organizations. Leaders must be adept at understanding what excites individuals to engage them in their work and garner their commitment to the organization (Davenport, 1999). Knowledge-based leaders should possess the skills to elicit and harness human capital.

THE ORGANIZATIONAL-CENTERED MODEL OF HUMAN CAPITAL

Traditional models of human capital acknowledge many of the same components of human capital as Davenport does, but these traditional models place more emphasis on crafting a positive organization climate rather than individualizing incentives for the "human capital investors." However, these traditional models continue to offer leaders tremendous insights on the behavioral aspects of human capital.

Traditional models suggest that the work environment should focus on enriching the individual. These models further suggest that leaders should craft strategies that link employee growth and performance to organizational goals. In general, their conclusions correspond closely with Davenport's human capital model. Harmony between the investor and traditional models lies in the underlying truth that successful organizations place emphasis on developing human capital capabilities prior to the generation of high returns. The traditional human capital models identify key principles for leaders seeking to build high-performing organizations (Crutchfield, 2000; Dess & Picken, 1999; Pfau & Kay, 2002):

- Develop a clear vision of future organizational needs and link knowledge and human capital needs to the vision.

- Understand current knowledge and human capital capabilities versus required future capabilities. The gaps between current and future capabilities should be mapped and closed.
- Develop an environment where the stakeholders have a vested interest in success and a role in developing the future vision.
- Hire, develop, recruit, and retain based on organizational needs.
- Use human capital gap reduction strategies to propel the organization from the current to ideal state.
- Stress accountability by providing a collegial and flexible work environment but tie these privileges to organizational needs.
- Develop knowledge-driven results by using quantitative and qualitative benchmarks to assess performance.

STRUCTURAL CAPITAL:
TIES THAT BIND THE ORGANIZATION

During the Industrial Revolution, organizational leaders and economists were bedeviled by the problems associated with diminishing marginal returns—or "too many cooks spoil the soup." Diminishing returns result when an organization adds more resources to a process, and returns associated with those resources grow fast initially and then begin to slow, eventually going flat. At some point adding more resources may actually reduce the returns—too many unproductive resources begin to interfere with the productive resources. During the 19th and 20th centuries, the law of diminishing returns applied to all forms of capital. However, in the late 20th century and continuing into the 21st century, knowledge-rich products and services began to defy the law of diminishing marginal returns. The overt and planned use of knowledge demonstrates that products and services can continuously evolve through innovation and invention.

How is it possible to achieve continuous increasing returns? Organizations experiencing this phenomenon achieve it by adding new knowledge to products and services before diminishing returns sets in. Knowledge advantages are too numerous to fully list them all; however, a few examples include enhanced market intelligence, improved customer resource management, technology advances, and enhanced manufacturing. Knowledge is the renewable resource that changes everything. Smart leaders target the full range of human capital capabilities to allow innovation and creativity to flow to the aid of the organization. The linking of people to the organization is accomplished through structural capital.

Structural capital is the "plumbing and wiring" that links humans to the organization (Dess & Picken, 1999). Since structural capital links the organization and people, it should also be viewed as a key leadership variable in order to set human capital free to power growth. Structural capital links individual tacit knowledge to explicit organizational knowledge through technologies, processes, culture, and procedures. This form of capital amalgamates organizational activities to facilitate learning and goal attainment. By defining, and optimizing, structural capital, the organization takes a leap toward knowledge-based leadership.

MAPPING HUMAN CAPITAL NEEDS

Linking human capital to the organization requires a thoughtful and structured approach. It also requires a great deal of collaboration within the organization to breakdown department or functional silos. Concept mapping allows leaders to connect concepts, ideas, needs, and capabilities to develop knowledge strategies (Jonassen & Yacci, 1993; Novak, 1991). This notion of mapping can be applied to link human capital to structural capital as well as the needs of the organization. In Figure 5.1, a human capital mapping tool is illustrated.

The human capital map identifies the key strategic, operational, and functional requirements required by the position. Typically, only key employees that influence the organization are identified. The identification of human capital requirements through the mapping exercise is intensive. Accordingly, the organization will need to make decisions on how extensively it will use the mapping tool.

Strategic levels define big picture plans within the organization; operational levels are the multifunctional processes in the organization where services and products are delivered; and the functional level is typically related to functions of the organization such as finance, operations, or information technology and the like. Many organizations do not adequately define human capital needs associated with all three organizational levels of planning and operations. Since recruiting is the "big bang" associated with human capital management, undefined human capital requirements may lead to recruiting and hiring practices that do not meet the critical needs of the organization.

Identify required human capital abilities as shown on the left-hand side of the knowledge map. This establishes the critical characteristics that define full competency for that position. Be certain to list behaviors such as ethical standards and emotional intelligence characteristics required, as well as knowledge and skills essential for the position. Establish the incumbent's current "stock" of human capital to provide a baseline on the right side of the map. The human capital gap is then the difference between the incumbent's current stock of human capital and the position's required human capital.

Care should be taken in establishing the human capital skills such as cognitive skills and knowledge. It is important to be specific by identifying knowledge to achieve success at the strategic, operational, and functional

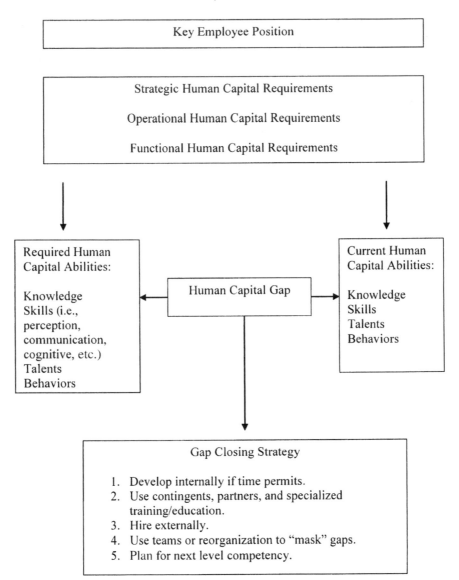

Figure 5.1.   A Human Capital Mapping Tool

levels characterized by level of knowledge (i.e., know-what, know-how, know-why, or care-why). Thinking may include dimensions such as critical evaluation, problem solving, creativity, reflectivity, as well as the ability to think in collaborative environments. Communication and social skills should be equally well-defined and tied to organizational needs.

By fully defining the human capital characteristics, the human capital gap has meaning for the leader, employee, and organization. Achievable organizational strategies can then be selected to help mask shortcomings from required human capital components. Since no individual is a "perfect" fit, it is quite normal to find "gaps." The map should be a "living" document modified for changes in the external and internal environments. By continuing to link organizational needs to human capital needs, the organization is seeking to optimize all forms of capital. It makes no sense for an organization to invest time and resources to do cash budgeting, financial budgeting, capital budgeting, and market planning to optimize financial and physical capital to "meet mission goals" and then ignore the primary capital: human capital.

EXAMPLE OF DEVELOPING A HUMAN CAPITAL MAP

To provide an example of human capital mapping, let us consider the dilemma a community goes through when hiring a new school superintendent. With all of the problems facing local school systems, hiring the top administrator has become complex. Let us suppose that our fictitious community, a small city of 35,000 residents, is located in the northern plains region of the United States—the agriculture belt. The community is steeped in production agriculture with little economic diversification. Additionally, the community faces an aging and declining population base. In an attempt to stem youth out-migration from the community, the school board recently changed the mission of the school system to provide a quality comprehensive education steeped in vocational skills, participation in workforce development, and engagement in community development. The prior superintendent was a long-term teacher and administrator in the district nearing retirement age. The superintendent felt that her skill set did not match the new mission and decided to take an early retirement. The school board must now construct a position description to hire a new superintendent who can engage the community and make the mission a living vision for the community.

The human capital mapping exercise will not only create a road map for hiring, but it will also help the school board in understanding that the optimal candidate will not fully possess all of the required human capital abilities—there are no perfect fits in the real world. The map also helps the board members understand what resources will be required to assist the new superintendent in fulfilling the mission.

What are some of the human capital capabilities that will be required? Functionally, the new superintendent will need to understand kindergarten through high school education requirements and other governmental education requirements. The superintendent will also need to be skilled in student and teacher development methods. These items were the core requirements for the prior superintendent. However, with the new mission, the operational and strategic ability levels will be quite a departure from the past. The new human capital requirements should be listed on the left-hand side of the map.

What are a few of the new requirements? Since the new superintendent will serve as a focal leader in workforce and community development, a few of the important human capital abilities may include

- a firm understanding of the economics associated with rural farm communities;
- an ability to craft human capital development strategies to meet new industrial clusters in the community;
- the capacity to serve as a change agent in the community and the tenacity to remain positive during the period of change.

List the key operational and strategic abilities. Now, under each of these abilities list the knowledge (know-what, know-how, know-why, and care-why) requirements for the position. Also list the required skills (communication, tact, empathy, etc.) associated with these complex abilities. Finally, list the behaviors (professional, confidentiality, ethics, and so on) that will be required. Fully flesh out the lists of key human capital requirements for this position. As the candidates are evaluated, list their current capabilities on the right-hand side of the map. The difference between the required and current capabilities represents the "gap." Select the best candidate and then use the gap closure strategies to help the new superintendent fulfill the challenging responsibilities of the position. For key positions, mapping exercises are central to improving the potential for "hiring right." For incumbent key employees, the same exercise should be completed—develop a gap reduction strategy for incumbents too.

CRAFTING AN UNDERSTANDING OF HUMAN CAPITAL FROM OTHER DISCIPLINES

Leadership theory owes a debt of gratitude to psychology, sociology, anthropology, economics to name but a few intellectual fields of contribution. A major theme in intellectual circles is the integration of knowledge from all sources to craft working solutions. Insightful leaders seek wisdom from all sources to harness the creative power of humans. Some of the less "mainstream, " but exciting, psychologists such as Howard Gardner of Harvard University are introducing ideas about the nature of human performance that bear examination. Gardner (1993) introduced the notion of multiple intelligences and individualized education to optimize an individual's strong suit. Gardner's theory has significant implications to the notion of human capital. As one considers the dimensions of human capital, the notion of multiple intelligences possesses considerable potential in identifying and developing—as well as categorizing—human capital for an organization.

Gardner makes keen distinctions between what some psychologists consider intelligence. Some believe standardized aptitude test scores provide a generalized intelligence quotient (IQ). Still others suggest that the speed of answering test questions is a predictor of intelligence. Gardner (1993) breaks with this tradition and defines intelligence as "the ability to solve problems, or to fashion products, that are valued in one or more cultural or community settings" (p. 7). The seven forms of intelligence identified by Gardner include linguistic, logical-mathematical, spatial, musical, bodily kinesthetic, interpersonal, and intrapersonal.

Gardner believes that in modern society linguistic and logical-mathematical forms of intelligence have dominated education sectors; however, the ability to be "successful" after formal education is highly dependent on the use of the other five forms of intelligence by an individual. This notion of multiple intelligences suggests a dimensioning, or expansion, of human capital characteristics formed along the lines of multiple intelligences.

Most forms of "multiple intelligence" are defined by title, but a few deserve explanation. Spatial intelligence is formed by the "ability to form mental models of a spatial world and to be able to maneuver and operate using that model" (Gardner, 1993, p. 9). Spatial intelligence is dominant in professions such as engineering, medicine, and art. Bodily kinesthetic intelligence comprises using one's body to solve problems or the physical dimension of work. Individuals high in intrapersonal intelligence are skilled at self-awareness, assessment, and management. Some consider intrapersonal skills akin to metacognition.

Viewing the dimensions of human capital through the multiple intelligence framework adds texture to human capital management. Adding these dimensions to the mapping exercise provides additional criteria to evaluate human capital fit, development, and engagement within an organization.

CONCLUSION

To some, human capital is a fuzzy notion that belongs in a human resource or training department. This approach is a mistake. Line supervisors and colleagues have more to do with human capital development than any other department. No doubt there must be an accounting of human capital within an organization and the human resources department can fulfill this accounting need, but there must also be accountability for human capital development and deployment. The primary human capital responsibility lies within the leadership of an organization. Successful leaders tie human capital to organizational needs, identify sources of human capital, and develop human capital (Tobin, 1998). Linking organization learning, knowledge acquisition and application, and human capital to a successful strategy can never be the responsibility of a "staff department." These important tasks are not sidelines to a leader's responsibilities, but they are how a leader fulfills his or her responsibilities. What is the real product of a successful leader? People do the things required to succeed; leaders quite literally lead people to success.

During the era of capitalism, society well understood how to use physical and financial capital combined with labor to grow the bottom line. But in a competitive knowledge society, machines have largely replaced labor. People at all levels of an organization are knowledge assets, or human capital, and this is an organization's competitive advantage. Certainly leaders must tend to financial and physical capital concerns, but the paramount concern must be the full integration of human capital into the organization's plans for success.

SIX

STRUCTURES FOR SUCCESS: STRUCTURAL CAPITAL

The intangible duty of making things run smoothly is apt to be thankless, because people don't realize how much time and trouble it takes and believe it is the result of a natural and effortless unction.

—A. C. Benson, excerpts from the letters of Dr. A. C. Benson to M. E. A.

Successful leaders tackle the most thankless but highly important task of structuring an organization to use knowledge. The structural links within an organization that lead to organizational success include leadership capabilities, organizational structures, as well as culture. Some organizations, to their detriment, overlook the importance of these structural linkages. The value of organizational linkages has grown in importance and is now known as the *structural capital* of an organization. Consider the importance of simple linkages in everyday life. A chain is only as strong as its weakest link. A door is only as strong as the hinge. And so it is in an organization—an organization is only as strong as its links.

Structural capital includes the processes, procedures, culture, organizational hierarchy, and information systems that links people within a business and connects them to their suppliers and customers (Dess & Picken, 1999). Basically, the "things" that make an organization run that are not already accounted for in physical, financial, intellectual, or human capital are considered structural capital. This form of capital is the glue that binds an organization, and once bound it is highly resistant to change. Consider your own habits developed over a lifetime. The practices are well rehearsed and assist you in getting through a day. In fact, much of what you do daily is akin to a form of individual structural capital—you would not make it through a day if you had to think and attend to every detail. Structural capital for an organization works very much the same—it helps an organization get through a day without thinking about every detail.

An organization's structural capital should be designed and tuned to its vision, mission, and knowledge needs. No matter how energetically a leader attempts to engage an organization in knowledge-based change, if the structural capital is not in harmony with the change, the leader is doomed to failure.

THE COMPOSITION OF STRUCTURAL CAPITAL

An easy way to define the structural capital in your organization is to start with a distinction. Simply list external and internal relationships. For instance, customer, client, supplier, and partner relationships certainly are part of structural capital. How an organization is viewed by external constituents (i.e., customers, governmental agencies, suppliers, and the like) is also part of an organization's structural capital—in other words, your organization's reputation is structural capital.

Internally, an organization's values, culture, philosophy, ethical standards, systems, procedures, information management control and reporting systems, and just about anything else that links value creation in an organization are part of its structural capital. Leaders must not only understand these important components and their architecture within an organization, but know how to engineer changes within the structural capital as well.

An organization is a chain of capital components, and structural capital is the linking mechanism in the chain. Anyone knows that you cannot ride a bicycle driven by a chain that is missing a link. Well, a leader cannot implement change in an organization that is missing a link. It really is that important. In every organization, structural capital is unique. No consultant can provide the "winning" recipe. Leaders must sort out the right approach within their organizational constituents. By understanding the nature of structural capital, a leader can implement the necessary changes to optimize people and knowledge as competitive advantages.

Individual knowledge and capabilities—human capital—matter very little to an organization if it cannot collectivize these capabilities and improve the organization (Stewart, 1999). The ability to collectivize individual knowledge and make the "output" of knowledge tangible is a central function of structural capital. A leader must be able to articulate what structural capital is, define what it looks like in an organization, and know how it works or does not work. The leader must take the fuzzy connections, write them down, and write down how they work. If you cannot fully articulate a concept, then you cannot change the concept.

Thomas Stewart (1999), an important intellectual capital researcher and author, concludes that structural capital is more important than human capital in knowledge organizations. He points out that many categories of structural capital are entitled to the rights of ownership and can be patented, copyrighted, and protected under trade laws (i.e., technologies, inventions, data, publications, process, and strategies).

PROCESSES, POLICIES, AND PROCEDURES

Processes are critically important to an organization. Without processes, organizations would never produce products or provide services. Processes are so central to value creation that companies such as Kentucky Fried Chicken and Coca-Cola take great pains to protect secret recipes and production processes. Many organizations work diligently to structure their processes to meet stringent international quality standards. The International Organization for Standardization, commonly known as the ISO, is one of the international organizations that provides certification of organizational processes. ISO 9000 certification focuses on quality management and quality assurance standards, and ISO 14000 focuses on environmental management issues.

Travel globally and look at billboards or glance through international trade publications. Many international organizations tout their ISO certification in these advertisements. These leading organizations know that customers recognize the importance of processes and process quality. Proven and consistent processes represent value to customers, so smart organizations also pay attention to processes.

Policies, processes, and procedures clearly define an organization, and when combined with branding, they are worth money. Why else would someone pay a premium for a McDonald's or Arby's franchise? Why do Sylvan Learning Centers command a premium? Because consumers have made a decision about the products and services they offer and value the consistency of the product. The knowledge of an organization is enshrined in these products through the structural capital of an organization.

We typically do not worry about the average intelligence of a teenage pizza delivery person when we order a Domino's pizza. The collective marketing, process control, defined ingredients, and methods of making and delivering the pizza are not dependent on the IQ of the delivery driver or the person who tossed the dough and put on the ingredients. The quality of the pizza is to a large extent the collective knowledge and capabilities of Domino's organization—Domino's structural capital.

CULTURE MATTERS

If policies, procedures, and practices matter, and they do, they form the backbone of explicit knowledge and structural capital in an organization. Culture defines the environment for interpreting and implementing policies, procedures, and practices. Culture is the inheritance of an organization that determines the shape and content of policies, procedures, and practices. Leadership success and the structure of knowledge in an organization are tied to culture. Culture can lift a leader through change or serve as an anchor weighing down any attempt to affect change.

Historically, organization success was viewed as being resource based. Culture was linked to the development and preservation of internal resources. Research results now suggest that knowledge, not merely resources, is the key competitive advantage and most organizations are now knowledge based (Boisot, 1998; Grant, 1996; Teece, 1998). The new economy is not a new information or technology model, but it is a knowledge-based model (Hewlett, 2000). Arguably, the new economy is really the knowledge economy, and it is enhanced or stifled by cultural influences. Culture in most organizations is still tied to a resource model and is not suited to a knowledge-based model. Culture has a profound effect on the structural, human, and intellectual capital of an organization. Culture is a learned phenomenon and it influences workplace matters such as team composition, acceptance of change, and employees' perspectives.

There is an abundance of evidence that culture is transmitted from one generation to the next (Bisin & Verdier, 2001). In families, traditions—culture—are passed down from parents to children. In organizations, traditions and expectations are learned from one generation of workers, and leaders, to the next. The transmission of culture is sustained through an adaptation and imitation process. Bisin and Verdier (2001) explain the persistence of cultural trait transmission through the mechanism of socialization via imitation and learning from role models. Their model suggests that in organizations, role models are powerful agents for transmission of culture within an organization. In news organizations there is the lore about the crusty old editor who disdains computers and only uses a typewriter for copy. So cub reporters try to emulate the crusty editor and they too use typewriters—the modern newspaper is driven by computers and so must the next generation of reporters. Typewriters in modern newsrooms only slow down the process of getting the paper to print. These ancient machines diminish quality by adding time to processing articles and requiring additional resources for necessary editorial collaboration and story verification. However, the cultural lore of the old editor dies hard, not only in news organizations, but likewise in all organizations.

If the leadership legacy within an organization reflects an appetite for an open-minded exploration of ideas, encourages knowledge acquisition and sharing, and uses knowledge to transform the organization, chances are good that these knowledge-friendly cultural traits will dominate. Alternately, if organizations are rigid in structure, driven toward resource minimization, and reward knowledge hoarding, it is a good bet that these cultural traits will dominate. Bisin and Verdier find that culture and preferences are highly resilient to change.

Preferences in an organization are bound by culture, which in turn frames hiring decisions, succession planning, policy creation, and procedure development. Developing fanciful mission, vision, and value statements that run counter to organizational culture have little chance of reshaping an organization. The change in an organization must begin with leaders courageous enough to change an aged culture and develop an environment conducive to transformation. Effective charismatic leaders are adept at reading the "cultural environment" of an organization and working within the parameters of the possible as they seed change (Bryant, 2003).

Only a naive leader, which suggests that this person is not a leader at all, would attempt to overhaul an organization without understanding the cultural advantages or hindrances resident in the organization. Figure 6.1 highlights some of these linkages.

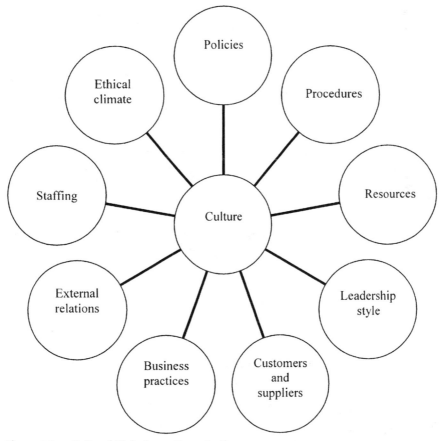

Figure 6.1.   Cultural Links in an Organization

To change an established culture from knowledge resilient to knowl-edge accommodating is not an easy task. A quick review of Figure 6.1 reveals the ties that bind an organization. Unfortunately, if an organization's cultural model is causing failure, then the model must change, and that is a major undertaking.

STRUCTURAL CAPITAL LEADERSHIP CHALLENGE

How does a leader change the organizational climate, culture, and ethics to enhance the structural capital of an organization? Well, no single answer can cover the myriad ways a leader can impact an organization, but research and practice do provide some important insights into this leadership challenge.

Leaders must establish the cultural benchmark and model the desired cultural traits. Leaders not only "talk-the-talk," they must also be capable and willing to "walk-the-walk." Leadership throughout the organization must be consistent to help the organization adopt the new culture. Leaders must establish standards, practices, rewards, and incentives that support the desired culture (Gilmartin, 2003). It makes no sense to suggest that knowledge acquisition, sharing, and usage are important and then implement a rigid and controlling management system that creates a disincentive for knowledge sharing in an organization. When people feel threatened or undervalued, they "clam up" and knowledge sharing ceases. Consistency and insight into the sociological and cultural aspects of an organization are essential leadership ingredients in crafting change. Mixed messages create a drive to the bottom not the top in a knowledge culture. If leaders set a culture of rewarding the "lone wolf" in an organization, then hoarding tacit knowledge will be the norm at the expense of collaborative knowledge sharing. Collaborative knowledge sharing adds to increased explicit knowledge development and enhances the organization's structural capital.

Current knowledge-based leadership research focuses on two key elements of leadership style: transformational and transactional elements (Bryant, 2003). Transformational leadership is "active" in crafting change. The leader motivates, inspires, and provides the intellectual stimulation to craft cultural accommodation (Hunt & Conger, 1999). Transformational leaders possess, and leverage, charisma to create change and encourage individual responsibility for problem solving and innovation. Transactional leadership refers to the technical process of making knowledge use efficient and effective. Effective knowledge leaders are capable of harnessing the charismatic elements of transformational leadership as well as the deep understanding of the nuts-and-bolts elements of transactional leadership. Understanding the nuts-and-bolts elements is essentially mastering the nature of knowledge.

Leaders are compelled to deal with the "soft" stuff in an organization that forms the composition of structural capital. The nature of status in an organization is a powerful cultural transmission structure (Bisin & Verdier, 1998). Bisin and Verdier studied the preference for "social status" in families. They analyzed the intergenerational transmission of cultural traits. By comparing parents' and offsprings' desire for social recognition, they were able to draw conclusions about social status in families that also hold true in organizations. They were looking for the stability of habit formation—or cultural transmission of values—from one generation to the next. They found amazing stability in the intergeneration transference of individual preferences or the transmission of social recognition and status.

The Bisin and Verdier (1998) study has important implications for organizations. If a younger worker takes over the position of his or her retiring mentor, there will be an expectation that the younger worker will attain the same social status and power of the retiring worker. Expectations are built upon this transmission device. An uninformed leader who attempts to interrupt these expectations, based on powerful desires for social recognition, may well doom his or her own initiatives—including knowledge initiatives. Knowledge initiatives are among the easiest to sabotage in an organization—all employees must do to sabotage knowledge growth is not offer up what is currently unknown in the organization but known to the employee. The nonsharing employee is at little or no personal risk.

The research suggests that with new expectations, leaders must be willing to provide compelling reasons to implement new expectations into the organization. Leaders who merely look to the next generation of employees to change the face of the organization may be in for a big surprise. A prime example of this resilience to change is the failure of legacy airlines in the United States to affect meaningful organizational change over the past 20 years. Many of the legacy airlines are now involved in chronic bankruptcy, while new upstart airlines such as Southwestern and Jet Blue have emerged with organizational cultures and business models that generate customer value and profits. The legacy airlines complain that existing union agreements, aging fleets, and unprofitable routes prevent them from modernizing their business models. These complaints prove the assertion that culture, employee expectations, and old models of status are resilient.

ADAPTIVE ORGANIZATIONS AND LEADERS

Edgar Schein (2004) suggests that leaders must become prepared to contend with perpetual change, and it follows that difficulties will arise from perpetual change because organizations are typically crafted around the notions of stability and routine work. Schein highlights the truth of industrial age culture, noting that it was designed around mass production efficiency and, in some cases, contractual labor obligations. Organizations with inherited cultures from the 19th and 20th centuries feed on stability, not perpetual change. Schein identifies two aspects of culture that need to be addressed in an organization: content innovation and role innovation. Content innovation is concerned with the ability of an organization to craft new services and products based on new ideas. Role innovation is framed by new approaches to doing things in an organization.

Content and role innovation are found in organizations skilled in adapting to or adopting a culture that blends technology, humans, and organizational structures that are conducive to perpetual change, adaptation, and innovation. Schein identifies several dimensions of organizational culture that are found in good learning and innovating organizations:

- An organizational view founded on the belief that organizations and its members control their destiny and success—they are proactive rather than reactive
- A pragmatic rather than philosophical or moralistic approach to reality and truth
- A near-term future orientation rather than a short-term or long-term orientation
- A belief in the individual and an assertion that humans are basically good and can be trusted, leading to a collegial and participative organization
- A unity or "connectedness" of subcultures in an organization

Organizations that believe in humans do not "overcontrol" them in their daily activities. Unnecessary overt control breeds contempt, not knowledge sharing. Job engagement and organizational commitment are high in organizations that are forward leaning, visionary, and collaborative. Empowered organizations focus on problem solving and improving the organization. Organizations that lack empowerment in the knowledge economy tend to be dysfunctional and littered with promises turned to failure.

Organizations that are dysfunctional must be gradually transitioned to functional learning organizations, and this takes time. Quick fixes only lead to the next crisis. During this period when transition must be the primary focus of the leader, a little weeding must take place before seeding new growth. Too many books and articles on organizational leadership and knowledge-based schemes discuss establishing idealized states of organizations without talking about the hard actions that the word *transition* implies.

Individuals and groups that hinder a culture of innovation and learning are poison to an organization. In this poisonous environment, some tough leadership calls will need to be made. Remember the Watson Wyatt (Pfau & Kay, 2002) findings about the rates of return on human capital. Hiring the right human capital, including the ability of the individual to fit into and assist in crafting a healthy organizational climate, represents the highest return on human capital available to the organization.

STRUCTURAL CAPITAL AND SOCIAL NETWORKS

Social learning, culture, and social networks are woven into the structural fabric of an organization. Individuals learn and replicate behaviors borrowed from their social networks (Bandura, 1977; Cross, Abrams, & Parker, 2004; Vygotsky, 1962). Knowledge—the practical knowledge that drives innovation and organizational advancement—is gained through social interactions guided by social networks. These social networks can be both internal and external. External networks include professional organizations, academic affiliations, and community affiliations.

Leaders can establish and positively influence social networks by encouraging and displaying an environment of trust, consistency, use of teams and collaboration, and role definition to facilitate interaction (Cross, Abrams, & Parker, 2004).

CONCLUSION

Structural capital is the glue that binds the organization, but in most instances it is "intangible" glue that creates tangible results. Structural capital represents the highly important matrix of an organization that is typically taken for granted. Good leaders optimize capital, and optimizing the structural capital is time consuming but absolutely essential to an organization.

Optimizing capital sounds like a straightforward proposition, and when one is discussing physical and financial capital, even human capital, there are metrics and benchmarks that provide a roadmap (i.e., rates of return, usage, opportunity costs, and the list goes on). But how does one optimize culture, social interactions, or even policies and procedures?

Classic problem-solving techniques provide insights into the structural capital optimization process. No problem can be solved before the problem is defined. Accordingly, the first step in enhancing structural capital is to inventory an organization's structural capital. What are the policies and procedures, and how do they support the vision, mission, and strategic objectives of the business? Write them down and link them to create an understanding of the entirety of their affect on the organization. In short, map what they are and how they affect the organization. The same mapping activity can be completed for intangible social factors of an organization. Mapping and linking social factors to effects in an organization make the intangible tangible. Leaders need to assess and identify the culture, social networks, rewards, incentives, and disincentives and their effects inherent in an organization.

Next, use a collaborative process to identify an idealized structural capital to support the organization vision. Evaluate the structural capital of competitors, partners, and other organizations. Borrow good ideas and tailor them to your organization.

Determine the gap between current and idealized structural capital. Note that there will be elements of structural capital missing and other elements that do not really seem to fit the organization. This is fine. The enhanced structural capital and gaps have now been identified. Leaders can take real action to fill in the gaps and reshape structural capital to meet the mission of the organization. Identification, mapping, evaluation, comparison, and action are major steps in optimizing structural capital.

Study the recommended changes—additions and subtractions—to the structural capital and "game it out." Build courses of action on how the recommended changes will affect the organization. Do the effects move the organization closer to the idealized organization? Leaders should be consciously attempting to uncover the effects from the law of unintended consequences.

Implement the changes, assess their effectiveness over a predetermined period of time, and solicit formal and informal feedback. Use the feedback to tailor structural capital. Remember, when leaders are tinkering with structural capital, they are tinkering with humans and culture—it is "soft science" stuff and precise mathematics and scripting do not govern outcomes.

The real returns on structural capital are measured in terms of other forms of capital. As structural capital is enhanced, the returns and effectiveness of human, intellectual, physical, and financial capital are enhanced. The hidden costs of failures in structural capital are witnessed in other areas of the organization. All forms of capital work together to boost organizational effectiveness, and structural capital links these multiple forms of capital for effective interplay.

SEVEN

WHAT SHOULD A KNOWLEDGE ORGANIZATION LOOK LIKE?

Knowledge of the first-rate gives direction, purpose and drive: direction, because it shows what is good as well as what is bad; purpose, because it reveals an ideal to pursue; drive, because an ideal stirs to action.

—Sir Richard Livingstone, *On Education*

The idea of structuring, or restructuring, an organization to effectively use knowledge can seem overwhelming. Where does one start? What should one do? How can it be done? These seemingly simple questions can freeze a leader if they are not put into perspective and framed by a model. Many call this perspective and model development process planning, some strategic planning, and others simply aligning an organization. Different organizations refer to this process in slightly different terms, but no matter what the process is called, planning is really straightforward. Basically, it consists of simple steps. It is not as difficult as some pundits claim.

Let us begin with a basic truth—there is no perfect organization and no two organizations should look exactly alike. Here are a few more principles that provide leaders with guiding wisdom as they build knowledge organizations:

1. The leaders and members of an organization must understand why the organization exists. This statement or concept seems elemental, but many people hold misguided views about the purpose of an organization (i.e., solid organizations understand that profit-driven businesses exist to earn profits, governments serve citizens, and not-for-profits fulfill their missions).
2. All stakeholders in the organization must be aligned to a common purpose and vision. Everyone must understand their organization's "lighthouse" principles—principles that guide an organization when the "environment" seems dark or foggy. The purpose and vision of an organization serves as a lighthouse beacon to light the way for stakeholders.

3. The resources of the organization must complement its purpose and support the vision of the organization.
4. There is no substitute for excellence in leadership. The wattage of the light in the lighthouse is established through leadership. Great leadership means a bright light and poor leadership, a dim light. The members of an organization may find it difficult to find a dim light in the fog—poor organizational alignment.
5. Organizations are living entities, not static organizational charts. Leaders need to care for organizations much like a family—relationships change over time and need to be renegotiated.
6. Leaders must possess an intimate understanding of how knowledge and capital affect the organization. This is the technical aspect of organizational leadership.

Read any management or leadership book and no matter how sophisticated the ideas, the bottom line is simple—thoughtful and insightful planning, decision making, and execution produce results. The problem with strategic and operational planning in most organizations is that it is done because someone in the organization was told to do it. Naturally, they revert to vague and generalized planning guidelines from a book, or class notes from a master's of business administration class, and then proceed to put their organization through a tortuous process of strategic planning.

If organizational leaders merely gather their members together and just talk among themselves, the simple act of communicating will produce some positive results. And so it is with strategic planning. Yet so many of these extensive exercises never seem to garner the predicted results. Leadership fads and the never-ending cycle of "programmed reinvention" consume attention without yielding sustained improvement. Does this process seem familiar? Hopefully not, but the hyped "leadership tool" that is easy to implement and then leads nowhere is an all-too-familiar scene. Thoughtful leadership is knowledge leadership, and it requires a deep understanding of the principles of working with people and capital, and linking the two in a common purpose—no substitutes, no quick fixes, and no formulas. Upper management is littered with quick-fix wizards who pitch elixirs of excellence, but organizations are buffeted from meaningful, and sustainable, progress by the never-ending "programmed fixes." Over the past quarter century only a handful of firms sustained excellence. One of these companies, General Electric, not only sustained excellence, but leaders from this company are highly sought after by other organizations.

THREE KEY PHILOSOPHIES FOR PLANNING

During the summer of 1976 at Fort Knox, Kentucky, at the tender age of 17, I was introduced to Senior Drill Sergeant, Sergeant First Class (SFC)

Jurado. SFC Jurado was a grizzled veteran of the U.S. Army and served as an infantryman in Vietnam. I was a mere basic training private intimidated by this imposing figure, but during the intense eight and a half weeks with SFC Jurado, I learned a great deal. Two gems of wisdom imparted by this special man have stayed with me and guided me during my military, business, and education careers. I do not know the origin of these gems, but they really hit home with me. Let me share them because they provide a terrific framework for planning and organizational success.

The first enduring lesson imparted by SFC Jurado goes something like this: "Hope is not a plan." I can still hear him bellowing this out as he asked how we were going to accomplish a task. This thought-provoking statement, although we did not have much time to reflect on it at the time, was typically followed by the lecture that "even a bad plan executed with vigor will do better than no plan."

What did SFC Jurado mean? The meaning is fundamental: Organizational members must know precisely what they are to do within an organization without constant contact with one another. Hoping that everyone will just "get it" and "pitch in" in a useful manner is folly. Planning is a purposeful process of organizational alignment.

The second important philosophical lesson from SFC Jurado sheds light onto what it takes to craft a successful organization. It runs counter to current Western society popular culture. SFC Jurado succinctly captured the lesson. He constantly told pesky complaining privates that "fair is a place where one rides rides and eats cotton candy." When young soldiers complained to SFC Jurado about the fairness of the task they drew, SFC Jurado reminded them about the notion of fair.

Organizations must do what it takes to meet the needs of their constituents, or customers, or they will not exist for long. Certainly honesty, ethics, and honor must be lighthouse principles, but everyone has different notions of fair, and an overt indulgence of "fairness" can foster an environment where organizations are twisted in ways that prevent them from being effective.

SFC Jurado was not implying that being arbitrary, impulsive, or compulsive is acceptable—he was merely stating the obvious: Everyone must pull his or her own weight, and more, in an organization to achieve the desired outcome. Good leaders create an environment where everyone understands how his or her knowledge and efforts foster value. Leaders also provide rewards for results that link people to organizational results. Failure to provide these links results in organizational fuzziness that fosters the "fairness" complaint.

Many fledgling organizations fail because leaders fail to establish practical organizational purpose. The majority of businesses that populated the Fortune 500 at its inception half a century ago are not on the list today. The reasons for these shifts are basic—leaders and organizational members forgot why they existed, or never really understood why they existed.

Aerospace is one of the key global industries. The use of knowledge has always been a dominant trait of aerospace companies. The real giants in the aerospace industry understand that their purpose is to provide aircraft that meet the needs of the airline companies' customers. Insightful and innovative aerospace executives comprehend that airline companies are in the customer service business—not just the transportation business. Understanding their organization's underlying purpose helps these thoughtful leaders guide their businesses to thrive, even during bleak downturns in the industry. These savvy leaders craft organizations that use the power of teams, knowledge, and innovation to reduce airline operating cost, enhance aircraft durability, and improve aircraft serviceability. These knowledge organizations embed knowledge of not only aircraft design, but also knowledge about the needs of the flying public into the design, manufacture, and service of their products. These leaders were knowledge leaders well before the term became popular. All leaders are well served to understand their organization's purpose, but if it is possible they should also understand the purpose of customers at least two levels above them—their customer's customer.

Education leaders must understand whom their institutions serve. Is it the student, who in many cases does not have the experience to evaluate the context of their education? Do they serve the parents who pay tuition or the communities that subsidize the institution? Can it be that education institutions serve the organizations that hire their graduates? Understanding who is served makes a major difference in how an educational institution is structured and how resources are employed.

Nonprofit organization leaders face the same daunting questions as education leaders—whom do we serve and why should we exist? Funding, resources, human capital, and other structural questions turn on these important questions. Certainly, profit-oriented businesses must adroitly address these critical questions or they simply cease to exist—the market is a hard arbitrator. But in the end, governments, nonprofits, and educational institutions also face the market—the market for donations and subsidies.

In all organizations, the issues associated with knowing who is served are critical to existence. Survival issues such as cash flow, ability to recruit and retain talented employees, and the ability to structure an organization that can innovate and adapt to change hinge on having an intimate understanding of the who, what, when, why, and the how of an organization. Gaining these important insights, and understanding them, leads to key lighthouse principles for the organization. Remember, the lighthouse is the beacon that shines for all to see, even in the dark and fog of life. Lighthouse principles serve to align organizations both internally and externally.

THE MISSION

If an organization already exists, a good starting place in answering the vexing existence question emanates from customers, clients, and constituents. Talk to customers and see how they think the organization is doing. Ask them how you can enhance your service or product to meet more of their needs. Ask the customers if there is anything else your organization can provide that may be of value. It is amazing that an organization will twist itself into knots for almost inconsequential new funding opportunities and ignore the core source of funds—customers. For instance, at many educational institutions the amount of funding provided by federal organizations can be a small percentage of total revenue. But that small amount of funding often controls the actions of the whole organization. Many state-funded universities and colleges receive less than half of their funds from state sources, but the state controls 100% of what they do and whom they serve. Private schools accept some restricted donations that are small relative to their total funding, but the donations may impart global requirements on the institution. Primary and secondary schools in the United States are locked into this same pattern of marginal funding that entails maximum control.

To understand if this funding-control scheme makes sense, leaders must fully understand why they exist, what the costs and benefits are, and what the alternatives are. Most importantly they must understand their mission. Many pundits have a slightly different take on what should be in a mission statement, but there are some generally accepted basic questions essential to consider in constructing the statement (Scarborough & Zimmerer, 2000):

- What does the organization value and what are its core beliefs about customers, employees, and constituents?
- Who are our customers, stakeholders, and clients?
- Whom do we serve and why?
- What do our customers want?
- What service or product do we provide and why do people want it?
- What generates our cash flow?
- At what quality level do we seek to provide services or products?
- Do we face competition?
- Who do we depend on beside customers for our existence and what are their expectations of us?
- What should we look like in the future to be relevant?

Honestly answering these questions is a critical step in crafting an effective mission statement. Before answering these questions do the research.

Ask customers, competitors' customers, partners, suppliers, owners, and employees these questions and reflect on their candid responses. The responses to these questions develop the schematic for the lighthouse. Do not forget to sneak a peek at mission statements from organizations in the same field. Developing a mission statement that fits an organization is a knowledge acquisition process, pure and simple.

Analyze demographic and market trends to understand the future needs of the organization. It does not take a rocket scientist to organize the data and draw some inferences. Do not trust your intuition alone—do the research and invite others into the process and be prepared for revisions. The final mission statement should be a simple and clear statement of why your organization exists and at what level it should exist (i.e., local, regional, national, or global). Consider the mission statement as a critical knowledge alignment device for your organization. It is the magnetic needle of the organizational compass that suggests what type and amount of capital is required by the organization to succeed. The mission statement also puts the "stake in the ground" as to what constitutes success. If the leadership team states that the lofty goal is to be recognized as the best in the world at what you do, then there it is—success is to be *recognized* as number one in the field. Setting unrealistic standards that cannot be achieved can do damage, and setting standards of success that are too easily achieved can destroy motivation and achievement in an organization. Be realistic in establishing the mission statement, but "lean forward on your leadership toes" in establishing a mission with a near-term future orientation. Also, keep the mission statement brief and to the point. The statement should consist of no more than a few sentences that are easily understood by all.

A sample mission statement helps illustrate the point: We will maintain market leadership in developing (providing, producing a certain service or product) through the effective use of cutting-edge knowledge, our people, and innovation provided at the highest quality and value. In this simple statement the world is informed that this organization will maintain a market leadership position by leveraging knowledge and human capital at industry-leading quality standards. The organization also states that it will compete on a value proposition, not the "lowest price."

Alternately, an organization may have a statement that suggests a different organizational stance: We will provide products (services) at the lowest possible price and guarantee complete customer satisfaction by offering a 110% price refund guarantee if our customers are not fully satisfied. This statement suggests that providing point-of-contact customer satisfaction is key to this organization's competitive strategy and low price is central to the strategy. Whatever an organization states as a mission becomes a bedrock lighthouse principle. Leaders do not violate the mission or tolerate violation of the mission statement. If an organization competes on service, then drive the organization to provide service. If an organization competes on low price, structure the organization to be able to always offer the lowest price. Wal-Mart competes on low price and inventory turnover. Wal-Mart has mastered the science of retail pricing and inventory management to fulfill its mission. Look at Wal-Mart's website or visit one of its stores and look at what they post near their name: "Always low prices. Always." Wal-Mart defines who it is, how it competes, and how it serves. Look at Wal-Mart's financial data for any year in the past 10 years and compare it against other major retailers. Its net profit is high, and it is high because of inventory management and turnover driven by low price. Wal-Mart has successfully structured its business around its core beliefs and mission statement.

While crafting a mission statement, many organizations will also develop vision and values statements and use them as guides for the mission statement. The vision statement paints a rich picture of what the organization must look like in the future to be relevant and successful. The value statement clearly announces the values of the organization: people, ethics, the environment, the customer, or other elements of the organization's culture that defines what is valued.

Using a road-map metaphor to highlight the relationship between mission, vision, and values provides clarity on how these lighthouse markers work together to shape the organization. The mission is the road that a vehicle moves across (what we do and how we do it), the vision is the destination, and values are the road signs that assist in the successful navigation of the journey. Collectively, these statements provide alignment internally and externally for the organization. Keep the statements simple, basic, and understandable—the KIS principle (keep it simple). Peter Drucker (1999) got it right when discussing the role of mission statements in an organization:

> People want to know what their organization is here for and how they can contribute. It does not have to be fancy or overly verbose, but it has to be concrete. Don't expect a twenty-five-year-old engineer to embrace a list of financial objectives as a statement of mission. (p. 118)

EXPANDING THE PLANNING PROCESS

With a mission statement in place, leaders must turn their attention to broadening their planning efforts. Defining current capabilities of an organization is the next logical phase in building a successful knowledge organization.

The following steps are critical in assessing the organization from the basement to the apex of the planning structure:

Step 1: Evaluate the current organizational strengths and weakness filtered through each of the five forms of capital (physical, financial, human, intellectual, and structural) as well as leadership capability.

Step 2: Scan the external environment for opportunities and threats to the organization.

Step 3: Define the knowledge and capital that will be required to fulfill the mission and vision of the organization.

Step 4: Identify the "gaps" in leadership and capital between step 1 and step 3.

Step 5: Complete a courses-of-action analysis to close the gaps.

Step 6: Choose and execute a course of action to close the gaps.

Step 7: Establish a feedback loop to validate progress and assess setbacks.

Planning is a systematic process to develop a road map for progress. Good planning, and modeling, allows leaders to assess the organization's abilities to achieve desired outcomes. What differentiates this form of planning from other models is the integration of the five forms of capital in the assessment and planning process. Since leadership and the five forms of capital form the backbone for growth in a knowledge organization, they must be assessed holistically.

IDENTIFYING AND MANAGING GAPS

Identifying current and future states is not an easy task, but it is an essential task. Parents are constantly querying their children on what they want to be when they grow up. When the youngster states, "I don't know," the parent laments and states, "You must have a goal to focus your education." Interestingly, the parent is telling the child to plan and identify the gaps between where he or she is now and where he or she wants to be in life. Organizations are very much the same as the child and good leaders are like the parent, not forcing the child, but guiding the child. Children will change their minds many times and outside influences will cause deviations in their path, but by planning they are forced to think through what they want to do and consider the steps it will take to get there. It is "focus" toward a mission and "alignment" of capital and resources that are important in the planning process, not always the answer.

Many elements are outside the control of the organization such as the economy, political changes, changes in laws, court decisions, competitors' actions, and of course issues of death and incapacitation of key employees. These elements cannot be fully foreseen in the planning process, but risks associated with their potential occurrence can be identified during gap analysis and hedged against.

Gap analysis not only identifies known deficiencies in the organization, but by developing various courses of actions and "gaming" them through, potential risks can be identified. Attempting to imagine the unimaginable is critical in a knowledge organization. If key tacit knowledge is lost, what can be done? Are there strategies where teams can be employed to make knowledge explicit? By gaming through each dimension of capital and developing gaping strategies, organizations become aligned and proactive, and their risk of failing is minimized. Knowledge leaders prepare organizations for change and managing the gap is a central leadership responsibility.

It should be clear by now that thought leadership is not "controlling." It is guiding, visioning, aligning, structuring objectives and outcomes, decision making with collaboration, and preparing organizations for change. Too many organizations are burdened by leaders with a very narrow definition of leadership—one where control is central to their definition. Control is achieved through objective setting, aligning resources, and structuring the organization for success—not dictating. Dictating presupposes that the leader is omnipotent and omniscient.

Conducting planning and gap analysis varies from organization to organization and from industry to industry. Figure 7.1 highlights key actions for thought leaders in planning.

Planning is a knowledge- and leader-centric exercise. In Figure 7.1, knowledge is the key commodity in the planning exercise. Knowledge is the commodity used in defining the current organization and the cumulative knowledge that it will take to move the organization to the next level in the future. While the complete organization is necessarily involved in the planning process, it is the leader who provides the framework and impetus for the planning.

In the late 19th and early 20th centuries, August Heckscher was known as a leading industrialist. B. C. Forbes, who later started *Forbes* magazine, once referred to Heckscher as among the nation's leading industrialist. Heckscher (2000) believed leaders were so critical in the management and growth process of an organization that in 1923 he laid down five simple rules for leading an organization. These rules align amazingly well with the idea of knowledge-based leadership and planning.

Heckscher suggests that all organizational leaders must have a "thorough acquaintance with general business methods" (p. 155). Heckscher is stating that leaders must understand how capital is used within their organizations and know how they interact to establish a positive cash flow. Know your organization, why it exists, and how to sustain it.

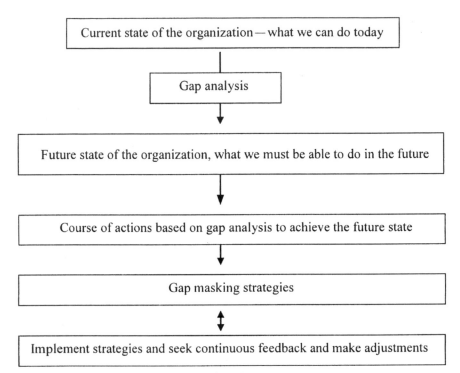

Figure 7.1.   Planning Implementation Flowchart

His second rule suggests, "If a competitor is selling or producing cheaper than you are, find out why and then shape your policy on the facts" (p. 155). Heckscher's statement is fundamental: know your competition and the opportunities and threats posed by the competition. Once again, Heckscher's second rule is a knowledge proposition.

Heckscher's third rule is based on the idea of structural as well as financial capital. He states, "If you cannot pay debts when they are due, fully explain why and preserve your credit" (p. 156). Existing organizations should fully understand their cash flow and have access to financial capital during periods of negative cash flow; however, fledgling organizations have "dry spells." During these periods, possessing a positive reputation, and good friend network, is essential in carrying the organization through the dry spells. Documented good planning is also important in supplementing cash flow from external sources during dry spells.

The fourth rule tells us that we should plan, analyze the plan, and then when something goes wrong—as it always does—cut the losses and move on. Heckscher states, "Do not nurse a loss. It is impossible to do business without now and again sustaining a loss. The big losses come from trying to avoid the inevitable—from hanging on to hopes rather than facts and thereby bringing on complications " (p. 157). Heckscher, much like SFC Jurado, did not place much stock in hopes.

There can be no substitute for understanding the organization, comprehensive planning, and constant scanning to move a learning organization toward success. Heckscher's fifth rule reinforces this concept: "When you are managing a business know its every detail and what everyone else in your field is doing. . . . An active manager must know absolutely what is going on" (p. 158).

In today's global, litigious, and fast-paced environment it is impossible for one individual to manage every detail. However, a smart leader understands an organization thoroughly and aligns it through lighthouse principles. The "knowing" is collective in an organization. The leader aligns knowledge for purpose. Crafting and linking knowledge and capital is the thoughtful leader's challenge.

Heckscher concludes his advice with a management cornerstone:

Experience quickly teaches which items are important and which are not and the time consumed in examining them is not nearly so great as might be imagined. . . . Management to me is essentially first knowing the principles of business and then applying them to the particular business in hand. (p. 159)

He is simply telling us to know, apply, and do.

Today all organizations are knowledge organizations. There is no substitute for knowing and using knowledge. Is the 21st century so different from the 19th and 20th centuries described by Heckscher? Not in principle, but certainly in practice. Some believe that technology has changed everything, but it has not—it only provides a tool to advance Heckscher's rules in the new century. As everyone uses the same technologies, no competitive advantage exists for any single competitor. What establishes the differences between successful organizations and those that do not achieve their missions is using the knowledge and capital of an organization to plan, link, and execute.

EIGHT

LEADERS SHAPE, NOT BEND, AN ORGANIZATION

Thinking always ahead, thinking always of trying to do more, brings a state of mind in which nothing seems impossible.

—Henry Ford, *My Life and Work*

To be effective, leaders must pierce resistance in an organization without causing undue callusing. Leadership is more about shaping an organization to fulfill its mission than bending organizational structures into compliance. Good leaders focus on the essential problems to be solved. Leadership is active, not passive; creative, not restrictive; empowering, not imposing; forward leaning, not demeaning. Leaders excite organizations to win through vision, planning, and follow-through.

Today, unlike any other time in the past, the domain of leaders is nestled in the seemingly intangible world of ideas and knowledge. Knowledge leaders must be capable of making the intangible tangible. Knowledge leaders work with people and people do not behave the same as physical or financial capital. Talk to a colleague about "optimizing him" and see how he reacts. People need to be involved in developing vision, planning for the future, and then they will engage. In a knowledge organization it is impossible to be an effective leader without being a people leader.

Here is the summation of this chapter: Leaders must be capable of "showing" an inviting future to achieve it. "Show," do not "tell," the future through action, written plans, concrete actions, and firm links to resources. The old story of "do more with less" wears people thin. Knowledge leaders are committed to using knowledge in new ways to create "more" from "more" knowledge: more work, more services, more products, more quality, through more knowledge. Effective planning and capital linking form the path to achieving "more." Remember, a two-pound bag of sugar only holds two pounds of sugar. Leaders use knowledge to produce a bigger bag.

The initial step in planning requires describing a concrete destination for the organization and clearly articulating its current location. The next step entails careful planning for the journey from the current location to the destination. The more detailed the plans, the fewer opportunities there are for surprises. The more adventurous will just begin the journey without proper planning. The more adventurous are typically rewarded with surprises.

Leaders are paid to avoid unwanted surprises—this is the managing aspect of their position. Leaders must also serve as myth busters. Planning is knowledge and fact driven, so even assumptions must be built upon facts. Leadership also involves developing a systems perspective. A systems perspective for knowledge-based organizations means leaders build the ability to execute change through the system, the five forms of capital, enriched by knowledge networks (Hooijberg & Schneider, 2001).

A good way to view the essential tasks for knowledge leaders is to look at what they lead. Knowledge leaders lead through affecting the efforts of people, visionary foresight, and the ability to make decisions from a systems perspective (Hamel & Prahalad, 1994; Katz & Kahn, 1978). When leading through knowledge, leaders must tap the social intelligence, or the collective wisdom, of an organization. Innovative leaders craft success; they do not rely on hope. If an organization becomes dysfunctional and unable to effectively employ knowledge successfully, then the leader must take the ultimate blame. Leaders are ultimately responsible for the results of their organization; organizations should not be held responsible for the results of their leaders.

Leadership is a privilege that entails personal sacrifices, insights, hard work, and risks. The leader is the sage on the stage and is watched closely. True leaders, by virtue of their positions, give up their rights to negativity and criticism. However, the rewards of leadership are many and no less tangible than those of an architect who proudly points to his or her latest high-rise creation. Leaders watch with pride as team members are empowered and take actions to erect the organizational "high-rise" of success. Knowledge leaders earn a rare respect from their colleagues when they get it right, and it is this type of deep respect that few experience in life.

GETTING IT RIGHT

The capacity to see and communicate the "big picture" as well as a "fruitful future" for an organization is the bedrock for leaders. Some refer to this leadership ability as visionary. But being "visionary" is more than charisma; it is tied to a leader's ability to conceptualize the organization from a larger scope, or context, within society. It is a learned cognitive skill. This essential leadership ability is also referred to as "systems thinking" (Senge, 1990, p. 185). System thinking requires forecasting, researching, and visioning skills.

These systems skills are honed by interacting in a knowledge-rich environment with diverse stakeholder groups (Hooijberg & Schnieder, 2001). Leaders must have confidence in their ideas, enough confidence that the leader will allow team members to debate and hone them. Good leaders collaborate with team members, so active debate only improves solid decision making. Naturally, leaders should think through their ideas with critical analysis and reflection before entering a collaborative discussion stage.

Leaders are ultimately responsible for making decisions, but shortcutting idea refinement is contrary to building a knowledge organization. By encouraging team member interaction to hone system thinking, leaders develop strong human management, motivation, and technical skills within team members that encourage commitment, loyalty, and the ability to manage the inevitable conflicts that arise from time to time (Mann, 1965).

Leaders who perform multiple tasks involving multiple roles tend to have a broader perspective and concept repertoire. Ultimately, these broad perspective leaders are judged more effective (D. R. Denison, Hooijberg, & R. E. Quinn, 1995; Quinn, Spreitzer, & Hart, 1992). In order for leaders to multitask, they must be willing to delegate authority, responsibility, and some decision-making capabilities to team members. Organizations populated by these types of multirole leaders are typically judged more effective. These conclusions concerning leader effectiveness are intuitive. Leaders who interface with multiple stakeholder groups through diverse tasks increase their knowledge of an organization. Leaders who are capable of building knowledge networks and learning organizations multiply their effectiveness. It just makes good sense.

These findings do not imply that leaders can be effective even if they are egocentric and lack good mentoring and relationship skills. In fact, just the opposite holds true; egocentric leaders often have problems cementing positive team relationships. Leaders must be more than merely skilled in relationship skills; they must also be able to envision an organization systematically to forecast needs. The idea that if one can lead and manage one type of organization, then one can lead any type of organization is misguided. Leaders must have sufficient knowledge, and skill, to engage in meaningful systems thinking specific to their organization.

BUILDING A COOPERATIVE KNOWLEDGE NETWORK

Senior leaders are unable to lead or know every aspect of the operations in their organization. Effective leaders not only tap into social and knowledge networks, but they also co-opt stakeholders to exercise legitimate power (Mitchell, Agle, & Wood, 1997). Co-opting is the ability to link opposing views into the larger group through negotiation and rightful compromise. For leaders to be effective, they must know "who" as well as "what" they need to know. Leaders must develop a knowledge network. This network building should be an early initiative for leaders intent on crafting learning organizations. But how is it done? How can the myriad of important linkages be defined for a leader? As always, it begins with simple exercises that prompt additional thinking.

Building a knowledge network list is intuitive. List all of the people who have knowledge or can inform decision making. Have team leaders add to that list and annotate the knowledge relationships. Continue to develop this list of knowledge sources. Knowledge network development should happen before, during, and after the strategic planning process. In short, the networking process is continual, and that is why strategic planning and visioning should also be continual.

To do something with purpose, one must be capable of articulating that purpose and delineating the actions to carry out the purpose. Simply put, one must be able to write down his or her thoughts in a cogent fashion to help shape those thoughts completely. The same principle holds true for building a knowledge network list. This is really a list of people and organizations that form the know-what, know-how, and know-why connections. Here are some recommended steps in developing the knowledge network list:

Step 1: Determine what knowledge is currently required for the organization to be successful today. Do this through inventorying knowledge requirements. Categorize the knowledge needs by the five forms of capital (financial, physical, human, intellectual, structural). Write down the required knowledge.

Step 2: Assess the organization's capacity to fulfill its vision along the five basic forms of capital. List knowledge and capital needs. This step links future knowledge requirements with current knowledge requirements. Add these knowledge requirements to the list.

Step 3: Invite members internal to the organization to assess the knowledge network. This is a collaborative step that allows others to voice knowledge needs. Add these knowledge needs to the list.

Step 4: Invite external stakeholders such as partners, suppliers, customers, clients, consultants, and board members—all individuals or groups external to the organization that have a vested interest in the success of the organization—to assess the knowledge network. This is not only a collaboration activity, but also represents a problem-solving step. Many external stakeholders may offer knowledge solutions that augment the organization's knowledge needs. Naturally, leaders must balance proprietary needs with knowledge sourcing needs when inviting external members to participate.

Step 5: Identify stakeholders to fill knowledge gaps and assess their willingness, and ability, to share tacit knowledge with the organization. Identify the depth of knowledge with respect to needs (i.e., novice, practitioner, or expert), and compare that knowledge depth to the organizational need. Gaps may still exist.

Step 6: Prioritize the criticality of the knowledge needs and define risks associated with not fulfilling certain identified knowledge needs.

Step 7: Begin to brainstorm sources of knowledge for the items still remaining on the list after step 6. This is the "formal" gap closure stage. Identify how the missing knowledge can be accessed by the organization (e.g., consultants, human capital development, hiring, additional partnering, etc.).

Step 8: Identify someone within the organization to be responsible for the maintenance of the knowledge network. Some large companies use a chief knowledge officer. Small companies designate the responsibility to an individual who understands the role of knowledge within the organization.

This list should be a "living" list that is adjusted with needs. The list can be as simple as a spreadsheet or as complex as a formal link in the organization's enterprise resource planning (ERP) system. The key reason in developing the list is to allow leaders to wrap their minds around their knowledge needs. The list can never be all inclusive, but it should inform the leader of the knowledge needs and who in the network can fulfill the needs. Knowledge lists identify the knowledge to enhance organizational products and services.

Many educational institutions take a simple look at their education resources by focusing solely on the teaching and administrative staff at the school. However, a bevy of knowledge and instructional resources are available to even rural schools, including civic leaders, parents, libraries, business leaders, and the list goes on. A hundred years ago, the extended community was expected to participate in the educational process of a community. Today, our communities have become sterile with silos of knowledge and skills. Knowledge organizations are knowledge communities where silos of knowledge dissolve into an alluvial mixture of capabilities.

Here are a few words of caution for leaders when developing a knowledge network list: Make sure that sources of knowledge are credible and founded on goodwill—sources should have a vested interest in the success of the organization. A wise leader understands the difference between stated and revealed preferences. Stated preference is what people say—and this type of preference is typically unreliable and unstable. Revealed preference is the outcome of what people do with precious resources such as time, money, and effort. Knowledge sources should be individuals, or groups, who have revealed a valid commitment to the organization.

A SYSTEMS APPROACH

What is a systems approach to knowledge and human capital management? It is a structured integration of knowledge with capital. What does structured mean? Structured implies that leaders, in collaboration with team members, undertake a step-by-step approach to analyzing the organization and then link mission, vision, marketplace, capital, and knowledge to form an integrated plan for success. Businesses would refer to this exercise as a business plan. Governmental organizations, schools, and nonprofit organizations should also develop the equivalent of a business plan that recognizes all five major forms of capital. Most business plans typically focus on market conditions and physical and financial capital, while only a few look at human capital. Most business plans do not explicitly recognize intellectual or structural capital.

A systems approach recognizes that explicit knowledge along with human capital form the pool of intellectual capital that generates solutions. A systems approach also acknowledges that knowledge sources and human capital assets will change over time. Identifying multiple sources of knowledge helps to diversify an organization's knowledge portfolio and prevents knowledge "walkout" when key individuals pursue new interests. Using multiple knowledge sources also provides for a portfolio of multiple perspectives in problem solving.

GOOD SOURCES OF HUMAN CAPITAL

Great leaders systematically identify sources of human capital for a whole organization. Because of the less tangible nature of human capital as opposed to physical capital, many organizations have been slow to identify and manage it as capital. Personalities, skills, knowledge, behaviors, talents, and past experiences all go into picking a winning team.

Leaders who have conducted a human capital mapping exercise for key employees can now use these maps to hone their knowledge inventory. The key to successfully inventorying human capital begins with a top-down perspective and then addresses specific human capital shortcomings with a bottom-up plan.

When looking at the organization from a top-down perspective, start with the mission and vision statements. Take a global perspective. For instance, based on mission, will the organization operate in an international environment? If so, understanding the culture, language, and local bureaucracies becomes an essential human capital ingredient for the organization. Also, implied in an international environment is the need for financial, procurement, and human resource professionals who possess knowledge and skills such as the ability to work in multiple currencies, consolidate financial statements, recruit employees, understand international laws, and so on. If an organization is involved in governmental operations, it needs people who understand how to link with affiliated governmental organizations.

Next, subdivide human capital requirements, and potential sources, down to the functional levels of the organization. With the needs assessment complete, identify from the bottom up the human capital currently available to the organization from all sources: employees, stakeholders, partners, suppliers, professional affiliates, and organizations—anything is possible. Use the human capital map and the knowledge network list to identify knowledge and human capital sources during the bottom-up analysis.

The required human capital skills identified in the human capital mapping exercise (see Figure 5.1) should be linked to the top-down organizational needs assessment. The skills identified on the right side of the map—current human capital skills—identify the stock of human capital available to the organization. Departments, functions, and partnerships can be reorganized to mask human capital and knowledge gaps.

This approach to masking gaps recognizes that the whole is in fact greater than the sum of the parts. Outsourcing functions is a form of masking human capital gaps. For instance, look at what it might take to recruit and develop human capital for a nonessential service or product within the organization. Many firms specialize in providing services to organizations, such as billing, accounting services, payroll, personnel recruiting and testing, technology services, customer resource management, and the list goes on. These firms are capable of developing human capital economies of scale and scope in providing state-of-the-art services. Many times the outsourced quality is high and the price less than in-house services.

An organization is only capable of developing and managing so much capital. Leadership and managerial talent can only be stretched so far. Outsourcing can be a strategic multiplier that maximizes the effectiveness of the organization. A word of caution about outsourcing: These partnering businesses must be viewed as strategic partners that control key portions of an organizations capital—intellectual and more. Competitor organizations may also use your strategic partners to augment their capital gaps. Relationships and contracts should be crafted with a firm sense of reality. Severability, security, and propriety of processes, procedures, and operational trade secrets should be explicitly addressed in contracts and the outsource plans (Nonaka & Takeuchi, 1995).

If an organization decides to use internal resources, then human capital gaps can be masked through the use of teams and contingent, or temporary, workers. Teams can be structured to collectivize knowledge. The use of teams can be beneficial for more than sharing knowledge—teams, constructed properly, can bring unique perspectives together to solve problems.

Choosing the method of closing knowledge gaps is tied to human capital sourcing. The ability of the organization to recruit, reward, and retain human capital is a limiting factor. There are varying levels of stability associated with how leaders choose to source knowledge and mask gaps. Identifying the level of stability or risks associated with closing the gap is important. Leader risk tolerance and option availability will also dictate the methods of knowledge and human capital gap closure.

LEVERAGING KNOWLEDGE AND HUMAN CAPITAL

Finance experts are highly skilled at identifying sources of financial risks and recommending useful forms of leverage. A good financial professional can measure the degree of operating leverage, financial leverage, and break-even points. They will also tell you that risk is cumulative: the degree of operating and financial leverage can be combined to determine the degree of combined leverage—a more comprehensive measure of leverage—for an organization (Brigham & Houston, 2004). These superb analytical tools give financial professionals and organizational leaders insight on the exposure of the organization to risk and leverage.

Human capital and knowledge can also be leveraged. This form of leverage and risk can be thought of in much the same manner as financial risk. Human and intellectual capital are forms of capital much the same as financial capital. Then why be less analytical about the organization's risk exposure associated with human and intellectual capital? Leaders should not be less rigorous, but how can human and intellectual capital risks be assessed? Evaluate risk by categorizing and assessing source and mission risks.

Mission risks are associated with organization type. If an organization is a janitorial service company or fast food restaurant, it will have less human and intellectual capital risks than a pharmaceutical company. The more dependent an organization is on key human intellectual assets to fulfill its mission, the more exposure an organization has with respect to mission risk. Attempting an exotic mathematical equation to assess this risk is meaningless. Leaders need to categorize this level of risk based on a low, normal, or high ranking.

Low-level mission risk organizations tend to have very formalized structural capital. In low-level mission risk organizations, a major portion of the organization's human and intellectual capital resides in headquarters operations. A major portion of the knowledge required of fast food franchisers is linked to corporate marketing programs and embedded in the equipment and procedures developed by the corporate headquarters. High levels of turnover do not disrupt fast food organizations. Low-level mission risk organizations are characterized by low wages, large turnover, very systematic structural capital, and knowledge embedded procedures. Due to these characteristics, many of the occupations within the organization are commoditized jobs (Schlosser, 2002). Commoditized jobs are process-rich jobs that require limited levels of training or insightful knowledge. Some argue that these jobs should be "automated." To a large degree, they have been automated, but a human is required to "service" the automation or push the broom.

Medium-level mission risk organizations are characterized by organizations steeped in manufacturing, midlevel service and sales, repair, maintenance, and many governmental agencies. Intellectual capital is embedded in processes within these organizations, but human capital adds equal value to processes. In medium-level mission risk organizations, a high degree of know-what and know-how knowledge is employed by people to fulfill the organization's mission.

High-level mission risk organizations are characterized by a high dependence on innovation and invention. These organizations must be capable of reacting quickly to change. High-level mission risk organizations are characterized by complex sales, technology-rich products, and customized services (e.g., accounting and law partnerships). Educational institutions, research organizations, professional organizations, military services, politicians, lobbying groups, and software companies are among the growing list of high-level knowledge-rich organizations. In these types of organizations, procedures and structural capital are aligned to people. Individuals with know-how and know-why knowledge capabilities dominate these organizations.

While there is a degree of subjectivity, leaders should be able to identify their organization's degree of mission risk. If your organization has a high level of mission risk, then identifying human capital gaps and sources is critical to mission success. Alternately, organizations with low levels of mission risk should spend more time analyzing financial, physical, and structural capital gaps. After determining the degree of mission risk exposure, an astute leader will determine source risk.

Source risk is the level of exposure associated with how human and intellectual capital is sourced. If all of an organization's human and intellectual capital is sourced internally through stable permanent employees with no gaps, then the source risk is low. Organizations that rely on teams and other internal masking strategies for capital have a medium source risk. Organizations that use high amounts of outsourced services, contingent workers, and partnerships and that consistently leverage external stakeholders to meet their required human and intellectual capital sources possess high-source risk.

The degree of source risk represents organizational leverage. If an educational institution uses a large number of "part-timers" or adjunct teachers, then it has a high degree of source risk. If a research firm uses an extensive amount of external research, then it possesses a high degree of source risk. Organizations with a high degree of source risk are potentially exposed to tacit knowledge "walkout" as well as economic risks. If the economy becomes "hot," leveraged human and intellectual capital assets may seek a degree of permanence by accepting new employment arrangements. This undermines the human and intellectual capital of the losing organization. The more an organization is self-contained in human and intellectual capital, the more resilient it is to economic fluctuations.

Combining mission and source risk highlights the exposure of an organization to human and intellectual capital leverage. Organizations that have high levels of both mission and source risk should build knowledge redundancies into their strategies. Remember, few organizations can afford to possess all of the desired capital. All organizations must accept tradeoffs between costs and risks. Some leverage is desirable and necessary to manage costs. However, just like financial leverage, too much leverage can be dangerous as the economic environment shifts.

LEADERSHIP IS MORE THAN INTUITION

Leadership in our competitive knowledge-driven global society is more than smiling, patting people on the back, and being highly intuitive. Knowledge leaders are analytical and strategic in building capital sources. Developing inventory and sourcing tools for human and intellectual capital is essential. Identifying risks and planning to eliminate unnecessary risk is good leadership.

Once organizations acquire the human and intellectual capital necessary for success, then nurturing of capital becomes critical. When an organization acquires physical capital, a maintenance schedule and budget are established. Why should human and intellectual capital be any different from physical capital? All forms of capital are essential to success and they require care and feeding.

NINE

THE CARE AND FEEDING OF KNOWLEDGE WORKERS

The chief obstacle to the progress of the human race is the human race.

—Don Marquis, *The Almost Perfect State*

We are now in the era of the workers called the cognitive class. These knowledge workers are transforming our communities, societies, and how value is created in organizations. Defining the attributes of the new cognitive class necessitates a brief historical look at capitalism. The new cognitive class requires leaders who can inspire and provide vision for the essential ingredients in the new capitalism. Unfortunately, much of our modern practices in education, government, and organizational management are rooted in the traditions of early capitalism.

In early industrial and agricultural capitalism, the workers provided the care and feeding of the land and machines. Today, owners and managers must provide the care and feeding of knowledge workers that form the backbone of the new cognitive class. Knowledge workers are the transformational and value-creating agents of the new economy. Leaders must learn how to maximize this value, and that will require a serious rethinking of what constitutes value, capital, and ownership.

To facilitate the new ways of viewing workers, focus and reflect on the three key themes of this chapter: Capitalism is the dominant successful model of economic organization; our institutions and social practices are products of archaic forms of capitalism and need to adapt to new economic realities; and the definition of management and leadership must adapt to knowledge value creation.

CAPITALISM IS ALIVE AND WELL—JUST DIFFERENT

The long-winded debate over whether capitalism as a positive form of economic organization has run full circle. In the later part of the 18th century, a Scottish moral philosopher, Adam Smith, singularly combined several disparate concepts of capitalism that had been peculating over three previous centuries. Specifically, Smith suggested that private ownership of economic entities was good, pursuing rightful self-interest was good, and the means to accomplish the greatest production of goods and services rested in the division and specialization of labor (Smith, 1991).

Smith laid out the manifesto for laissez-faire—free market—economics. Others articulated portions of the manifesto prior to Smith, but Smith clearly and comprehensively made the case for capitalism. This notion put the owners of capital squarely in the economic driver seat. Smith was part of what we now call the classical economic tradition and a principal architect of the Scottish Enlightenment. David Hume and Thomas Paine shared this enlightened natural rights movement of the 18th century. The Enlightenment sketched the scene on the blank nascent intellectual and political canvas of the newly created United States. Capitalistic traditions inherited from England and Europe provided the rich texture and color to the sketch.

During the era when Smith wrote, the state owned a great deal of the productive capacity of a nation—the land—and maintained sovereignty over the people. Labor was wantonly wasted and misallocated by the state. Smith wrote during the eve of the Industrial Revolution. The capitalist during the Industrial Revolution took division of labor to new heights. Processes were reduced to their most elemental level, and it was during the 19th and 20th centuries that mass production took hold. The state no longer held sway, but the tactics of owners toward workers were not significantly different from those of the preindustrial period of state control. Workers were treated as mere cogs in the production cycle, a necessary ingredient to garner production from the machines and the land. The treatment of the workers as mere inputs to production led to dehumanizing excesses that were captured by the writings of Charles Dickens and other notable novelists as well as political writers. Dickens's great novel, *A Christmas Carol*, written in 1843, was a repudiation of Scrooge and capitalism. Classical tradition political writers such as Karl Marx seized on the negative byproducts of early capitalism to develop alternative utopian visions of economic organization—communism, where the workers owned all means of production. As evidenced by the 20th-century experiments with communism, humans tend to hinder others more severely in utopian worker-owned environments than do the profit-motivated capitalists. Communism failed and capitalism continued to evolve.

Western socialist political writers continued to dwell on the excesses of capitalist owners during the 19th century and the first half of the 20th century. The socialists equated exploitation of the worker with capitalism. Marx suggested that the central flaws of capitalism lay in the inefficiency of the modes of production, the exploitation of workers, and the alienation of workers (Marx, 1964).

Capitalism and political institutions evolved over the years to respond to the first two complaints of Marx: specifically, inefficiency and the exploitation of workers. The workers' movement in the early 20th century in Europe and the United States fostered labor unions as well as changes in laws that mitigated worker exploitation. The growth in global capitalism and the requirements for economic returns to attract additional capital ensured that only efficient organizations succeeded—the underlying principles of laissez-faire economics—the strong succeed and the weak fail, keeping the economy strong and vital. However, the issues of alienation of workers raised by Marx, the great German philosopher Hegel, and later writers such as Hannah Arendt (1958) continued to surface. What is this alienation of the workers and in what form is it manifest?

Simply, alienation is the separation of the human from the product of daily existence. As humans are removed from the product of their efforts and distanced through processes and procedures, they are alienated from the results of their creations, or as Marx stated, individuals become objects of their work. The point raised by Marx is critical in today's discussion about knowledge workers. Today value is created through new products, services, and new ways of organizing productive activities devised by innovative knowledge workers. The knowledge workers' creations are central to modern value creation, not a by-product. In alienated environments, humans become less essential to daily existence. In knowledge-driven environments, humans are central to daily existence. Humans own the knowledge capital that creates economic value. They are not servants to the physical and financial capital of past generations of capitalists.

Certainly, division of labor and the effects of the Industrial Revolution contributed to this sense of alienation. These unintended consequences of industrialization were driven more from a zest for efficiency than any attempt to alienate the worker. Also, workers were looked upon as labor to feed the machines. As machines have become more adept at feeding themselves and the world has evolved to a knowledge economy, the knowledge worker must be also be fed and cared for. The worker becomes a *knowledge capitalist*. Unfortunately, the transition to a more enlightened view of the worker-owner relationship is lagging behind the realities of the 21st-century global economy.

A NEW UNDERSTANDING OF CAPITALISM

In the 19th and 20th centuries capitalists were considered the owners of private enterprises and generally managers were lumped in with the owners. The Western style of management was derived from Smith's ideas of centralization and specialization—centralization of production, product and service design, and function. Leadership was designed to achieve maximum shareholder returns through the "factors of production" known as land, labor, capital, and entrepreneurship. Land, labor, and capital were inputs, where "stated" returns such as wage, rent, and interest were returned based on an input-output recipe. Entrepreneurship, or ownership, retained the premium or profit associated with risk taking and shrewd management.

The industrial era management practices were so powerful that it wove itself into our education system. We currently provide efficiency of education through mass lectures, multiple choice examinations, and other efficient, although not always efficacious, teaching methods. Nonprofit and governmental management mimicked industrial era management methods seeking high rates of return on "capital" employed. Pick up any good intermediate financial management textbook today and you will quickly note that the underlying assumption of modern financial theory is based on the stockholder wealth maximization model (Brigham & Ehrhardt, 2005).

There is nothing wrong with the analysis or the underlying assumption of maximizing shareholder wealth as an incentive to increase capital stocks. However, there is something very outdated about the assumption of "labor" as a mere input into shareholder wealth generation. There is also something wholly wrongheaded about the notion of the returns to labor as "wage." This is the language of industrial capitalism, not knowledge capitalism. Just as capitalism has passed through stages such as merchant, agricultural, financial, industrial, and now to its knowledge or intellectual phase, so too must the ways in which we view capitalism.

A capitalist is a person who has capital invested in a business (Braudel, 1985). Capitalism is an economic system characterized by private or corporate ownership of capital goods where economic value is created through private decisions rather than by state control. These private value-creating investments are governed by prices, production, and distributions that are determined mainly by competition in a free market. Viewed in terms of historical forms of capitalism, the entrepreneur or owner is central in the organizational value creation process. In knowledge capitalism, other central contributions to value creation must be recognized—specifically, the knowledge worker.

In historical capitalism, the owner provided the means of capital growth and hence profit; but in today's knowledge-dominated world, the knowledge worker provides the knowledge or intellectual capital to fuel value creation. This new paradigm requires a rethinking about how to harness the knowledge of the employee—who rightfully becomes a subordinate partner with the owner in the new knowledge economy.

THE KNOWLEDGE WORKER IS TRULY FREE

The notion of employee freedom envisioned with the onset of the labor union movement is now being realized through knowledge workers. As organizations become more dependent on knowledge workers to provide their important services and drive product development, knowledge workers are central to organizational growth. Workers are free to choose how they employ their valuable tacit knowledge. Know-how and know-why are key ingredients to organizational success, and the workers own these important ingredients.

But if the workers are the owners of the key capital required in today's society, what does this mean to owners and workers? It means that big changes are coming and there will be a redefining of the owner-worker relationship. Knowledge workers will share in the returns associated with the value they create and knowledge workers will define what those returns look like. Knowledge workers will look for wages, but many other attributes will also be keenly sought, such as quality of "place" in the work environment and flexibility of work place (Florida, 2002). Knowledge workers will define their workspace as they see fit. This is already happening in Silicon Valley and other communities driven by knowledge workers. Drive around the Silicon Valley businesses and you will see knowledge workers outside playing basketball on company-provided basketball courts or wireless workers communicating with colleagues as they enjoy a spring day. The workers define their preferred "place" for work and enjoyment and smart organizations realize their preferences.

Organizations that retain the bureaucratic vestiges of the Industrial Revolution will drive knowledge workers away to more flexible and inviting organizations. This commonsense, but overlooked, shift in the workforce can already be seen by the amount of employment growth in small single unit businesses in the United States between 1991 and 1996 (Acs & Armington, 2003). Between 1991 and 1996, employment in single unit businesses grew by 15.1% versus only 6.5% in multilocation businesses. The largest employment growth sector during this period was business services, encompassing knowledge-based sectors such as information and communication, where employment grew at 28.7%.

Entrepreneurial workers and small businesses are driving the new economy. These new workers are knowledge workers who bring their knowledge about services, markets, products, marketing, and customer service to the customer directly. To compete for and retain knowledge, workers, owners, and managers will need new strategies that allow active participation by the knowledge worker. The new cognitive class is evolving though generational cultural revolutions—demanding more independence, leading to knowledge interdependence as well as learning and work flexibility.

A NEW KNOWLEDGE REVOLUTION

The revolution in higher education can best be viewed through the presence of the University of Phoenix and other online, or virtual, universities. These new virtual institutions of higher learning focus almost exclusively on student teaching, not student and faculty research. They offer their accredited degrees via the Internet, allowing greater flexibility for working students. Employment will soon go through a similar shift. Demographic trends, where people move from rural to urban environments, will be reversed to allow people to live in rural environments and work there through technology. The virtual workforce is on the horizon. Rule-bound businesses, educational institutions, governmental agencies, and nonprofit organizations risk obsolescence unless they understand what the new knowledge worker wants. So what do workers want? They want flexibility, a sense of ownership in their work, and the ability to innovate or participate in intellectual entrepreneurship (Florida, 2002).

They want to reestablish their lives and shed the sense of alienation that has crept into their lives. They want to be connected to the results of their efforts—they want to know they make a difference. A decade ago, the average graduate student in the United States sought a master's degree in business. Today, the most popular graduate degrees are in psychology, health care, fine arts, and education (Top Twenty Graduate Degrees, 2004). The new workers are voting with their time and money. The next generation of knowledge workers is revealing their preference for careers that make a difference; just making a high wage no longer serves as the principal discriminator for a career. Adam Smith's 18th-century capitalism proposal was not a battle cry for absolute freedom but a call for "conditional" freedom based on commercial interdependence. Today, the knowledge workers have the opportunity for commercial independence, and that has significant implications for business owners and organizational managers.

KNOWLEDGE WORKER ACCOUNTABILITY

How do knowledge workers create value and how can leaders and managers hold them accountable? Knowledge workers create value through innovation and invention. Some of the innovation is by design, but other aspects are due to chance. Knowledge workers not only create new products through searching for knowledge and creating new knowledge, but also by developing innovative methods to finance and market new products and services (Baldwin & Hanel, 2003). Features of innovations by knowledge workers include new production techniques, new organizations, greater automation, new intermediate products, new product functions, new materials, new functional parts, new services, improved quality and working conditions, reduced lead times, costs savings, extended product range, and the list goes on (Baldwin & Hanel, 2003).

The partial list of knowledge-based innovations from above impacts all types of organizations, whether they are educational, for profit, nonprofit, or governmental. These inventions and innovations are the driving force of the new and old economy organizations worldwide. As more organizations harness the power of the cognitive class, remaining organizations must also harness this new capital elixir or run the risk of being left behind. The benefits of innovation extend to improved output, quality, profitability, and cost avoidance. Under the industrial model, managers checked worker throughputs and output as metrics of success. This is easy to accomplish when the output of workers is physical and manifest. But how can one measure, or hold an employee accountable for, knowledge work that involves innovation, invention, or creativity?

The answer does not lie in trying to calculate trumped-up rates-of-return calculations. Most innovation is collective, not individual. So how can one impute or divine the separation of knowledge inputs? One cannot. The answer lies in the establishment of achievable organizational missions and visions and accomplishing these missions. In many cases, the creativity unleashed by productive knowledge workers will go beyond anyone's imagination. Just look at the market values of Microsoft, Amazon.com, Yahoo!, and the like—how could one ever set a return calculation in advance for these types of ventures?

The real measure of success can certainly be measured by traditional measurements of profitability, meeting budget, output, and the like. But the real measure is based on how well product and service innovations allow the organization to fulfill its mission and vision. How does knowledge craft new variants of existing products and services? Holding organizations, departments, and individuals to task against mission and how well mission is accomplished is a much better measure of a worker than time spent in the office.

Ask knowledge workers what incentives they value, and they link pay, flexibility, and other desired incentives to the success of the organization (Schuster & Zingheim, 1992). Keep a portion of the employee's pay variable and link it to the successful achievement of the mission and vision of the department and the organization. Pay should be viewed broadly as those types of compensation variables that have value to the workers—and they can be offered cafeteria-style. These compensation variables can take many forms, but they include health benefits, workplace assignment—including homework assignments—salary, recreation opportunities, public recognition, promotion, and expanded opportunities for participation and learning. The key component is to offer what the knowledge worker wants and note that it will be different for different people. Restructure the employee-employer relationship to a partnership between owner-manager and worker-partner.

Link the success of the organization to the success of knowledge workers. Link the customer or client to knowledge workers' flexible compensation. For an educational organization, link student learning to faculty compensation. For a nonprofit organization, link successful service provisioning or mission accomplishment to the workers' compensation. For profit organizations, link workers' compensation with many facets of organizational growth such as profitability, expanded product offerings, customer satisfaction manifest through repeat purchases, and so forth. For governmental organizations, success has many components. Linking government knowledge workers' compensation to citizen satisfaction with services, innovation of service offerings, cost reductions, and a variety of other mission components reinstates the idea of a civil servant.

All too often in nonprofits and governmental organizations, compensation plans are bureaucratically predetermined based on wage scales. These wage scales are industrial era attempts at internal equity or other such archaic notions. All workers do not provide the same level of innovation, so why attempt to regulate mediocrity through standardized compensation packages? If mediocrity is the goal, stay with predetermined compensation packages, divorced from mission accomplishment or customer satisfaction, and mediocrity is what you will get.

Allowing the knowledge worker the ability to strive to move the organization to be number one in its field of endeavor is critical. Even if the organization lands at number two or three, allowing innovation to drive the organization to the number one slot is the energy behind private ownership. As owners share in the results, so too do the workers. Regretfully, in governmental, educational, and nonprofit organizations there are stakeholders but not owners. Why not make the workers the owners? Set them free to innovate. Allow knowledge capital and the power of knowledge worker partnerships to drive innovation and success. If the goal is to be number two or three, but not fourth, fifth, or last, then the organization is planning to be mediocre. This planned mediocrity is the enemy of innovation or creative knowledge use. It is not bad to be number two because the organization failed to make number one, but it is bad to plan to be less than number one.

CONSTRUCTING A CREATIVE CLIMATE

Crafting a climate for creativity is a dicey, but critical, component of the care and feeding of the knowledge worker. The key to success is taking an inclusive and minimalist approach (Florida, 2002). What do I mean by a minimalist approach? Remember that you are dealing with idea people, and they are all wired differently. What works for one may not work for another. Establish minimums for dress and workspace appearance, and provide for maximum flexibility.

If workers want to wear suits, let them wear suits. If workers are comfortable in blue jeans, then let them wear jeans. If a customer will be visiting and expects a style of dress, share this knowledge with workers and dress appropriately. Some knowledge workers work well in clutter, others need an open space. Design working accommodations that meet both needs.

Here is the real important piece—ask your knowledge workers what they want; do not assume anything. Ask them what is important and attempt to accommodate reasonable requests. Flexibility in work environment, hours, and tasks embraces the expectations of the knowledge worker. Set parameters on budgets and wide limits on flexibility that align with organizational requirements, and then let your cognitive workforce make their decisions. It works!

Take care—not all workers are knowledge workers. Many commoditized workers still feed the machine. Allowing the knowledge worker–type flexibility for this group of workers typically results in chaos. At a university, professors come and go to their lectures and meet students during their office hours based on prearranged schedules. Everything else is pretty flexible for these knowledge workers. In many cases, university professors are paid less than their professionally oriented counterparts, but it does not matter because they pride their freedom of thought and place. Most universities invest in cogovernance between the administration and the faculty members. Faculty have their say and input into their working and environmental conditions. The output of research and quality teaching is aligned to the mission.

Office hours and work rules are not aligning devices for knowledge workers; cogovernance and adherence to vision and mission are the aligning devices. Office workers, maintenance staff, and administrators at these educational institutions have regular office hours; the key knowledge workers—the faculty—have high degrees of flexibility and freedom.

UNDERSTANDING: THE KEY TO CONFLICT AVOIDANCE

The concept of conflict resolution is meaningless for knowledge workers. Conflict resolution is rooted in the owner-worker conflict mode typical of unionized environments. When people feed the machines and are treated as commodities of production, conflict naturally arises and can go away just as suddenly. However, in knowledge organizations, sharing of knowledge is based on trust and understanding—not conflict.

What leaders should be attempting to foster is a "nobody-in-charge system" of management (Cleveland, 2004, p. 19). Conflict arises in industrial era command and control systems of management. In the industrial era, change occurred, but it occurred at a pace where centralized management had the opportunity to retain gathered facts, deliberate, and coordinate an organizational response through a centralized command and control hierarchy. Most organizations are organized like this today. Most of our institutions, leadership styles, and organizations coevolved through the industrial era—they all fit in a mid-20th-century environment (Murmann, 2003). However, globalization and the resulting creative destruction process have changed the economic environment before our institutions, leadership styles, and organizations have had time to adapt (Cowen, 2002). Creative destruction is the process of creating new organizations, products, services, and processes through knowledge and destroying the old.

In the new knowledge economy, old command and control organizations are overwhelmed before they are capable of responding. New trust-based organizations built upon a consultative and collaborative style of owner-worker relationship are the type of organizations that elicit knowledge and human capital investment. These interactive and comingled organizations are designed to use knowledge to invent and innovate and respond to change.

As new forms of communication and technology add dynamism to the way we organize, knowledge relationships also change the way we organize. Encouraging sharing of tacit knowledge and collaboration are key ingredients for the new knowledge organization. Trust and understanding are central to this new form of organization. We are not moving from centralized to decentralized organizations; we are already there. The new knowledge leader must be able to work in an environment where ambiguity and low levels of control are the norm. The key to meeting the challenges of the 21st century is to build a dynamic organization.

Dynamic and decentralized organizations are characterized by personal initiative, cooperative behaviors, virtual organizations, committees, and networking with extended stakeholders (Cleveland, 2004). The organizations are punctuated with an "us" attitude where we work with each other rather than for someone. *We* accomplish a common mission, vision, and objectives through shared values and knowledge. *We* align to succeed. *We* work with a common bond for a common purpose. Clearly, conflict based on command and control styles of management play no role in melding a cognitive workforce.

The secret of success in developing knowledge organizations, and to successful knowledge-based leadership, is the integration of thinking and acting. Knowledge silos based on functional and cultural differences have no place in new economy organizations. Leadership must work diligently and consistently to foster a trusting environment. Failures and successes are shared and are part of the organizational learning process, and leaders must encourage and accept this process. Unacceptable conflict is centered on issues of control. Alternately, civil debate over ideas is desired.

Flexibility of ideas, control systems, environment, and solutions is the key ingredient to successfully linking knowledge workers to the organizational mission. But what happens, and it will, when some workers just want to be disruptive? Remove them. Participation in the knowledge workforce is voluntary, but if they cannot adapt and thrive in an open and flexible environment, then remove them from the process. If their knowledge is essential to the organization, find a way for them to contribute individually. If they are not essential to the organization, help them find a place of employment that better suits their needs.

Knowledge leadership is challenging, to say the very least. However, the rewards of personal and organizational growth can more than compensate for the challenges. Knowledge leadership is more like the quartermaster of the ship as opposed to the captain of the ship. The quartermaster must understand the journey of the ship and provide for the ship's resources so the captain can successfully navigate to the destination. Knowledge leaders need a keen awareness of the nature of knowledge, organizational goals, and how to identify and close capital gaps that scuttle the journey of the organizational ship.

Ten

Final Thoughts on Knowledge, Leading, and Success

There is an immense ocean over which the mind can sail, upon which the vessel of thought has not yet been launched.

—Richard Jefferies, *The Story of My Heart*

Leaders ultimately determine if an organization is built to succeed. Leaders cannot guarantee success, but they do develop and hone the organization. As the name implies, leaders must *lead*. Responsible leaders do not blame others for organizational inadequacies. Active leaders—and those working with them—will make enough mistakes so that there is enough blame to go around. Leaders build the organization, so if the organization is not built "right," it is the leaders who have failed.

Respectful leaders understand the knowledge, skills, talents, and behaviors that make up organizational human capital. They seek to reinforce and reassure organizational teammates and build greater human capital capacity. They also know when certain team members cannot benefit an organization. As changes in the marketplace are thrust upon organizations, then organizations must change. This means that just like some physical assets no longer fit in an organization after a change, some human capital may no longer fit. Good leaders recognize the need for respectfully "retooling" an organization's human capital.

Team members are watching to see that leaders do the right thing, but they want leaders to do it in a decent manner. Team members who no longer fit should have an opportunity to build their human capital to fit, or they should find an appropriate organization and relocate. Removal from an organization should be the last step, and it must be handled humanely. People will ebb and flow through an organization, and smart leaders never "burn a bridge." Leaders, from top to bottom shape an organization.

But how does a leader provide a top-down environment to support innovation, knowledge creation, and garner recognizable results? The answer is basic to leadership. Leaders nurture innovation, establishing strategies that employ knowledge, build teams that produce results, and they follow-up.

BECOMING INNOVATIVE

Every organization is faced with doing more to compete. This never-ending pressure is a constant in the dynamic global marketplace. Innovative practices, spurred by knowledge, transform organizations. Transformed organizations compete and force competitors to do likewise. The innovation process is evolutionary and endless. Innovation is simply the practice of using knowledge to create more, better, and less expensive goods or services. Innovation is the backbone of quality improvements. In order to focus innovation, it must be tied to an organization's strategy (Spanyi & Eibel-Spanyi, 2004).

Establishing and communicating the link between innovation, knowledge, employee self-interest, and strategy are essential steps in structuring a successful environment. It can never be stated too often: Improving results is why an organization seeks, uses, and enhances knowledge. The message must be compelling. It must link the external environment to individual self-interest within an organization. Stakeholders must explicitly understand their stakes and roles in achieving results. The communication must be varied, continuous, and encompass all stakeholders—employees, leaders, partners, customers, clients, students, and citizens. The communication must focus on how innovation will shape an organization.

Innovation strategies should be aggressive, but achievable, and they should "stretch" the organization. Actions must support strategy and innovation goals. This support means backing the plan with energy, capital, and patience to achieve the goals. Consistency between statements, strategies, and actions is essential to establishing an environment for success.

Establish outcomes and assessment methods to determine if an organization is moving toward desired results. Outcomes and assessment methods are benchmarks, and metric devices are tied to leadership planning. If organizations are not moving toward the desired outcomes, their knowledge, strategy, capital, and innovation are not aligned.

Structural capital of the organization may not be built to provide winning capital linkage for innovation. If this is the case, consider employing Stephen Shapiro's (2002) seven-step framework for innovation: rethink, reconfigure, resequence, relocate, reduce, reassign, and retool. These seven steps serve as a checklist for leaders interested in innovation. Here are a few useful leadership actions in building an innovative organization:

Action 1: Answer some basic questions to verify the organization's current status in Shapiro's seven-step framework. Are processes in place that require the use Shapiro's seven-step model? Are teams structured for innovation? Are teams skilled in the innovation process? Is there a cultural bias in an organization that rewards rethinking, reconfiguring, resequencing, relocating, reducing, reassigning, and retooling? If the answers to these questions are "no," then the structural capital of an organization is not built for innovation. Leaders can hire people skilled in innovation and build structural and human capital that support innovation, but these actions must be well thought out and explicit.

Action 2: Leaders should establish an innovation environment. Knowledge sharing, open inquiry, critical thinking, and risk taking are key ingredients to both knowledge use and innovation. Creative experimentation is the hallmark of good innovation knowledge companies. Accept failures as part of learning and bury egos. The blame game is the surest way to create a "duck-and-hide" environment in an organization. People who are fearful for their positions will not take risks and will seek to hide behind organizational bureaucracy. Bureaucracy is the enemy of innovation.

Action 3: Leaders should provide organizational road signs for staged creative development. Stop, yield, and do not enter signs work to align random traffic on a road. Organizations, as part of their planning process, should provide signs of what is and is not acceptable for innovation and risk taking. Clever leaders do not position organizations to risk everything on the throw of a dice. Design key stages for review of process, product, or service innovation. Review projects at the end of each stage to see if it still looks as desirable as once thought. In this manner, risk is reduced; innovation is encouraged; and a top-down system linking knowledge, innovation, learning, and success is established.

Action 4: Leaders should establish short- and long-term views of the organization. Some items such as cash flow must be managed on a short-term basis—without it, organizations cannot exist. However, results from innovation and the use of knowledge take time. There can be many starts and stops in the innovation process. Knowledge result indicators should align with horizons that are long enough to give the processes time to take hold. Leaders should display an innovation ethos within the organization.

TELL ME A STORY

Leaders can show the potential rewards from knowledge and innovation through the time-honored tradition of storytelling. Making future intangible rewards seem tangible enough today to encourage people to invest in the organization is a difficult proposition. Storytelling—or painting a vivid mental picture—is a way to make buy-in easier. Humans are inspired by stories of courage, touched by stories of compassion, enriched by stories with timeless values, and awed by tales of success. Humans learn through metaphors. Yes, statistics and pronouncements can catch our attention, but great novels and books inspire us. The proof is in the billions of dollars, pounds, riyals, yuan, and other currencies spent yearly on books and movies. Then why do leaders continue to attempt to inspire with statistics and rule through benchmarks? Because it is safe ground and appears scientific. Statistics are great for quality control and gaining a sense of proportion. Unfortunately, statistics measure past actions, leaders use knowledge to paint future actions.

Ancient wisdom that affects our daily lives is transmitted to us by way of metaphors and stories. Ancient sacred documents such as the Torah, Koran, Bible, and others transmit their timeless lessons through stories and metaphors (Borg, 2001). Shakespeare's works, the Greek tragedies, and other classical writings remain relevant to our lives today because the stories are timeless. They reveal truth about human nature and we recognize patterns valid today from these classical truths. Stories and metaphors are powerful knowledge transference tools that successful leaders tap.

METAPHORS AS LEARNING TOOLS

A metaphor is a comparative use of language that develops associations. It is used so an individual can "see something as." At times, truth cannot be literally stated because it defies easy description, so we use metaphors to connect that which cannot be easily described to something we understand. Metaphors, although not literally true, can express the essence of truth. Metaphors represent a top-down approach to knowledge. They establish an intellectual structure for new learning, based on an understanding of a shared cultural understanding of an existing concept.

Metaphors can also be used to summarize and clarify knowledge transmission. A recent article on change management makes clever use of a metaphor to summarize, clarify, and anchor key elements of change management (Mento, Jones, & Dirndorfer, 2002). The article is well written and focuses on comparing and integrating several change management models employed at a few major global businesses. The authors depart from traditional writing style and in their conclusion, they summarize their major points through the use of metaphorical storytelling. The authors tell the story of a ship preparing to make a perilous journey. At key points in the story they parallel essential lessons about change management. Even if one chose not to read the article, one could easily understand the major steps in change management just by reading the conclusion.

Metaphors effectively and briefly make a point. In another easily read one-page article, the author uses a horse training metaphor to crystallize four key elements of leadership (Hauser, 2000). Hauser believes the key leadership elements are vision, reality, ethics, and courage. By weaving the horse training metaphor through the article, the reader easily relates how Hauser believes these elements lead to greatness. A brief excerpt of the article makes the point.

> Imagine yourself as a horse trainer. Before a horse enters your arena, you've seen its great potential, and you have a *vision* of what it can become. Stand in the center and let the horse move freely in circles around you. Observe carefully, and accept the *reality* that the horse's natural instinct is to bolt. Motivated by the *ethics* of service to your subject, you approach from a desire to develop its potential. Have the *courage* to sustain your initiative—to stand at the center of the arena while the horse, powerful in its own right, gallops around you, sometimes bucking or charging. When the horse tires of being alone and senses your desire to help, it will give cues that say, "I want you to take the lead." And you do. (Hauser, 2000, p. 62)

Hauser, in a mere paragraph, catches the essence of the way these four key elements of leadership interact. Later, the author discusses the desire to intercede and help the horse but defers buoyed by experience in understanding that it takes patience to let the horse develop skills on its own. Everyone who has ever been thrust into a leadership position can relate to the elements and emotions stirred by the horse training metaphor—it is a powerful way to make a point.

Increasingly, the realm of technical research is linked to the commercial world. Metaphors are being used to link information and knowledge transfer between technology and business types (Mather, Bickford, & Fleising, 2004). Much like the horse training metaphor, animal metaphors are increasingly used in scientific circles to transfer knowledge to nonscientists without the use of cryptic symbols and jargon. Metaphors and stories must be carefully selected since they rely on "common" culture to effectively transfer knowledge. Since agriculture and animals are common global cultural elements, it makes sense that there is an expansion of animal metaphors.

FILLING IN THE BLANKS

Metaphors and stories build a compelling and enjoyable way to transfer knowledge. The use of these tools cuts across organizational and geographic borders to achieve the desired learning impact. Yet metaphors can miss the knowledge transference mark unless they are thoughtfully employed. Metaphors must connect on common grounds between groups.

Attempting to use a mountain climbing metaphor to build a knowledge case for a group of people who live on an isolated tropical flat island will probably fail. Additionally, the metaphor is a framing element for the bottom-up details. To gain comprehensive knowledge, details must later be added to the framing provided by the metaphor (Ritchie, 2004). The metaphor borrows structure from the known for leaders to frame the unknown (Forrai, 2003). But metaphors only provide structure. Leaders must ensure that detailed knowledge is added to the new structure to fully align the organization.

Storytelling and metaphor use are powerful in transferring knowledge and concepts, but care must be exercised to validate that metaphors implant the correct knowledge. In short, leaders should validate the understanding of the metaphor or story.

Consider the metaphor knowledge transfer process as an exercise in building a house. Leaders work with teams to blueprint the knowledge. They transfer knowledge to team members by constructing and communicating the metaphorical foundation and frame. The detailed knowledge links to the metaphor much like the wiring, plumbing, walls, and fixtures are attached to the house.

CONCLUSION

Thoughtful leadership is fundamental to organizational survival. The ability to transact globally has set loose new competitive forces. The competition is global and intense among education institutions, governments, businesses, and even nonprofit organizations. It is a competition for capital and market dominance that will determine the face of the 21st century and beyond. Governments are vying for relevance in the world. Higher education institutions are seeking to make their marks and many are just trying to survive. For education institutions, reputation and student performance are key ingredients in survival. Businesses seek to develop the next product, or service, that will reap huge profits and ensure their survival for at least a few more quarters. Nonprofits seek to be relevant and to serve.

Knowledge and human capital will determine the fate of these organizations. In fact, much of the competition among organizations of all types is based on gaining a competitive knowledge edge and recruiting the best human capital available. "Brain drain" in a community, or organization, spells disaster in the knowledge economy. Good leaders recognize this fact, and they build organizations that serve as magnets for cognitive workers. The age of knowledge capitalism is upon us, and knowledge is the currency.

Cognitive workers will continue to reap huge rewards for their knowledge. Communities composed of low-skill manual and commoditized labor will continue to see their market power dwindle along with wages. The emergence of knowledge as the key source of competitive advantage brings with it serious consequences for the new economy. Those organizations that can attract, harness, and retain cognitive workers will weather the storm well and write the history of the 21st century. Those organizations that fail to harness knowledge will be mere footnotes in the pages of history yet to be written.

Make the commitment to be a knowledge leader. Creative learning organizations use knowledge wisely. Learn to lead and align the organization's flock of cognitive workers. Like the graceful flocks of migrating birds, people can also be aligned. Not as graceful formations walking in unison, but aligned as graceful intellectual formations that work together for common purpose without fully understanding all of the structures that align them. It is a leader's principal responsibility to build aligning capital and structures for the flock.

REFERENCES

Acs, Z. J., & Armington, C. (2003). Endogenous growth and entrepreneurial activities in cities. U.S. Bureau of the Census (CES 03-02). Washington, DC: Center for Economic Studies, Bureau of the Census.

Amernic, J. (2003). The impact of human capital management on shareholder value. *Drake Business Review, 1*(1), 32–34.

Arendt, H. (1958). *The human condition.* Chicago: University of Chicago Press.

Bacon, Francis. (n.d.). *Francis Bacon, 1551–1626. Of truth* (para. 1–3). Retrieved July 11, 2005, from http://www.westegg.com/bacon/truth.cgi

Baldwin, J. R., & Hanel, P. (2003). *Innovation and knowledge creation in an open economy: Canadian industry and international implication.* Cambridge, UK: Cambridge University Press.

Bandura, A. (1977). *Social learning theory.* Englewood Cliffs, NJ: Prentice-Hall.

Becker, G. S. (1964). *Human capital.* New York: Columbia University Press.

Bisin, A., & Verdier, T. (1998). On the cultural transmission of preferences for social status. *Journal of Public Economics, 70,* 75–97.

Bisin, A., & Verdier, T. (2001). The economics of cultural transmission and the dynamics of preference. *Journal of Economic Theory, 97,* 298–319.

Blendon, R. J., Benson, J. M., Brodie, M., Morin, R., Altman, D. E., Gitterman, D., Brossard, M., and James M. (1997). Bridging the gap between the public's and economists' views of the economy. *Journal of Economic Perspectives, 11*(3), 105–18.

Boisot, M. H. (1998). *Knowledge assets: Securing competitive advantage in the information economy.* New York: Oxford University Press.

Boissiere, M., Knight, J. B., & Sabot, R. H. (1985). Earnings, schooling, ability, and cognitive skills. *American Economic Review, 75*(5), 1016–30.

Borg, M. J. (2001). *Reading the Bible again for the first time.* San Francisco: Harper.

Boulding, K. E. (1966). The economics of knowledge and the knowledge of economics. *American Economic Review, 56*(1/2), 1–13.

Braudel, F. (1977). *Afterthoughts on material civilization and capitalism.* Baltimore: Johns Hopkins University Press.

Braudel, F. (1985). *Civilization and capitalism 15th–18th century: The structures of everyday life.* London: Fontana Press.

Brigham, E., & Ehrhardt, M. C. (2005). *Financial management theory and practice* (11th ed.). Mason, OH: Thompson Southwestern.

Brigham, E., & Houston, J. F. (2004). *Fundamentals of financial management* (10th ed.). Mason, OH: Thomson Southwestern.

Bronowski, J. (1978). *The origins of knowledge and imagination*. New Haven, CT: Yale University Press.

Bryant, S. E. (2003). The role of transformational and transactional leadership in creating, sharing, and exploiting organizational knowledge. *Journal of Leadership and Organizational Studies, 9*(4), 32–44.

Chaffee, J. (2002). *Thinking critically* (7th ed.). Boston: Houghton Mifflin.

Cleveland, H. (2004). Leading and learning with nobody in charge. In M. L. Conner & J. G. Clawson (Eds.), *Creating a learning culture: Strategy, technology and practice* (pp. 19–34). Cambridge, UK: Cambridge University Press.

Cochrane, S. H. (1980). The socioeconomic determination of mortality: The cross-national evidence. In S. H. Cochrane, D. J. O'Hara, & J. Leslie (Eds.), *The effects of education on health* (pp. 3–33). Staff Working Paper 405. Washington, DC: World Bank.

Cowan, T. (2002). *Creative destruction: How globalization is changing the world's cultures*. Princeton, NJ: Princeton University Press.

Cross, R., Abrams, L., & Parker, A. (2004). A relational view of learning: How who you know affects what you know. In M. L. Conner & J. G. Clawson (Eds.), *Creating a learning culture: Strategy, technology, and practice* (pp. 152–68). Cambridge, UK: Cambridge University Press.

Crutchfield, E. B. (2000). *Developing human capital in American manufacturing: A case study of barriers to training and development*. New York: Garland Publishing.

Davenport, T. O. (1999). *Human capital: What it is and why people invest it*. San Francisco: Jossey-Bass.

Decker, P. J. (1986). Social learning theory and leadership. *Journal of Management Development, 5*(3), 46–58.

Denison, D. R., Hooijberg, R., & Quinn, R. E. (1995). Paradox and performance: A theory of behavioral complexity in managerial leadership. *Organizational Science, 6*, 524–41.

Denison, E. F. (1962). *The sources of economic growth in the United States and the alternatives before us*. New York: Committee for Economic Development.

Denison, E. F. (1967). *Why growth rates differ*. Washington, DC: Brookings Institute.

Derry, S. J. (1990). Learning strategies for acquiring useful knowledge. In B. F. Jones & L. Idol (Eds.), *Dimensions of thinking and cognitive instruction* (pp. 347–79). Hillsdale, NJ: Lawrence Erlbaum.

Dess, G. G., & Picken, J. C. (1999). *Beyond productivity: How leading companies achieve superior performance by leveraging their human capital*. New York: AMACON.

Dewey, J. (1910). *How we think*. Lexington, MA: D. C. Heath.

Diamond, J. (1999). *Guns, germs, and steel: The fates of human societies*. New York: W.W. Norton.

Douglas, J. (1930). Down Shoe Lane. In F. F. Murphy (Ed.), *Webster's Treasury of Relevant Quotations* (p. 557). New York: Granercy Books.

Dretske, F. (1988). *Explaining behavior: Reasons in a world of causes*. Cambridge, MA: MIT Press.

Drucker, P. F. (1999). The shape of things to come. In F. Hesselbein & P. M. Cohen (Eds.), *Leader to leader* (pp. 109–20). San Francisco: Jossey-Bass.

Ebenstein, A. (2001). *Friedrich Hayek: A biography*. New York: St. Martin's Press, Palgrave.

Florida, R. (2002). *The rise of the creative class; and how it's transforming work, leisure, community, and everyday life*. Boulder, CO: Perseus Book Group.

Ford, H. (1922). *My life and work*. Garden City, NY: Doubleday, Page, and Company.

Forrai, G. (2003). Epistemology and the metaphor of the book. *Interdisciplinary Science Review, 28*(3), 217–24.

Gallini, N. T. (2002). The economics of patents: Lessons from recent U.S. patent reform. *Journal of Economic Perspectives, 16*(2), 131–54.

Gaquin, D. A., & Debrandt, K. A. (Eds.). (2003). *The almanac of American education*. Lanham, MD: Bernan Press.

Gardner, H. (1993). *Multiple intelligences: The theory in practice*. New York: Basic Books.

Gilmartin, R. V. (2003, November 10). *Ethics and the corporate culture*. Lecture presented at the Raytheon Lectureship in Business Ethics at Bentley College, Center for Business Ethics, Waltham, MA.

Grant, R. (1996, Winter). Toward a knowledge-based theory of the firm. *Strategic Management Journal, 17*(Special Issue), 109–22.

Greenspan, A. (1999, November 1). *Economy based on knowledge overtakes economy of stuff*. Speech to the Gerald R. Ford Foundation, Grand Rapids, MI. Retrieved April 8, 2004, from www.destinationkm.com/print/default.asp?ArticleID=783.

Greenspan, A. (2002, October 29). *Education*. Speech during acceptance of the Stephen P. Duggan Award for International Understanding, New York. Retrieved April 8, 2004, from www.indiainfoline.com/nevi/edca.html

Griliches, Z., & Mason, W. M. (1972, May–June). Education, income, and ability. *Journal of Political Economy, 80*(3), S74–103.

Hamel, G., & Prahalad, C. K. (1994). *Competing for the future*. Boston: Harvard Business School Press.

Harrison, J. R., & McIntosh, P. (1992). Using social learning theory to manage organizational performance. *Journal of Managerial Issues, 4*(1), 84–105.

Hauser, L. (2000, November). Leading with horse sense. *Training and Development, 54*(11), 62.

Hayek, F. A. (1988). *The fatal conceit: The errors of socialism*. Chicago: University of Chicago Press.

Heckscher, A. (2000). Can good management be reduced to simple rules? In P. Krass (Ed.), *The book of management wisdom: Classic writings by legendary managers* (pp. 151–60). New York: Wiley.

Hewlett, R. (2000). A tale of two economies: The old and the new. *Tennessee Business, 10*(1), 3–5.

Hooijberg, R., & Schneider, M. (2001). Behavioral complexity and social intelligence: How executive leaders use stakeholders to form a systems perspective. In S. J. Zaccaro & R. J. Klimoski (Eds.), *The nature of organizational leadership: Understanding the performance imperatives confronting today's leaders* (pp. 104–31). San Francisco: Jossey-Bass.

Houston, J. E. (Ed.). (1995). *Thesaurus of ERIC descriptors* (13th ed.). Phoenix, AZ: Orynx Press.

Hunt, J. G., & Conger, J. A. (1999). From where we sit: An assessment of transformational and charismatic leadership research. *Leadership Quarterly, 10*, 335–43.

Jaffe, A. B., & Trajtenberg, M. (2002). *Patents, citations and innovations: A window on the knowledge economy*. Cambridge, MA: MIT Press.

Jeffries, R. (2001). *The story of my heart*. Seattle, WA: The World Wide School. Retrieved July 12, 2005, from www.worldwideschool.org/library/books/lit/Socialcommentary/TheStoryofMyHeart/Chap3.html

Jonassen, D. H., & Yacci, M. A. (1993). *Structured knowledge: Techniques for conveying, assessing, and acquiring structured knowledge*. Hillsdale, NJ: Lawrence Erlbaum.

Katz, D., & Kahn, R. L. (1978). *The social psychology of organizing*. New York: Wiley.

King, L., & Appleton, J. V. (1997). Intuition: a critical review of the research and rhetoric. *Journal of Advanced Nursing, 26*, 194–202.

Kuznets, S. (1965). *Economic growth and structure*. New York: W. W. Norton.

Langenscheidt's Pocket Dictionary. (1999). New York: Merriam-Webster.

Lasch, C. (1979). *The culture of narcissism: American life in an age of diminishing expectations*. New York: W. W. Norton.

Livingstone, R. W. (1944). *On education*. New York: University Press.

Luckman, C. World of Quotes.com. (n.d.). Retrieved July 11, 2005, from www.worldofquotes.com/author/Charles-Luckman/1/index.html

Mann, F. C. (1965). Toward an understanding of the leadership role in formal organizations. In R. Dubin, G. Homans, & D. Miller (Eds.), *Leadership and productivity* (pp. 68–103). San Francisco: Chandler.

Marquis, D. (1927). *The almost perfect state*. New York: Garden City Books.

Marx, K. (1964). *Economic and philosophic manuscripts of 1844*. New York: International Publishers.

Mather, C., Bickford, J., & Fleising, U. (2004). Unpacking animal metaphors for commercial relationships in the biotechnology industry. *New Genetics and Society, 23*(2), 187-203.

McKeough, A. (1991). Three perspectives on learning and instruction. In A. McKeough & J. L. Lupart (Eds.), *Toward the practice of theory-based instruction* (pp. 1–14). Hillsdale, NJ: Lawrence Erlbaum.

Mento, A. J., Jones, R. M., & Dirndorfer, W. (2002). A change management process: Grounded in both theory and practice. *Journal of Change Management, 3*(1), 45–59.

Mincer, J. (1958). Investment in human capital and personal income distribution. *Journal of Political Economy, 66*(4), 281–302.

Mitchell, R. K., Agle, B. R., & Wood, D. (1997). Toward a theory of stakeholder identification: Defining the principle of who and what really counts. *Academy of Management Review, 22*, 853–86.

Monk, L. R. (2003). *The words we live by: Your annotated guide to the Constitution*. New York: Hyperion.

Moykr, J. (2002). *The gifts of Athena: Historical origin of the knowledge economy*. Princeton, NJ: Princeton University Press.

Murmann, J. P. (2003). *Knowledge and competitive advantage: The coevolution of firms, technology, and national institutions*. Cambridge, UK: Cambridge University Press.

Nonaka, I., & Takeuchi, H. (1995). *The knowledge-creating company: How Japanese companies create the dynamics of innovation*. New York: Oxford University Press.

Nosich, G. M. (2001). *Learning to think things through: A guide to critical thinking across the curriculum*. Upper Saddle River, NJ: Prentice-Hall.

Novak, J. D. (1991). Clarify with concept maps: A tool for students and teachers alike. *Science Teacher, 58*(7), 45–49.

Ormrod, J. E. (1999). *Human learning* (3rd ed.). Upper Saddle River, NJ: Prentice-Hall.

Paris, S. G., Cross, D. R., & Lipson, M. Y. (1984, December). Informed strategies for learning: A program to improve children's reading awareness and comprehension. *Journal of Educational Psychology, 76*(6), 1239–52.

Paul, R., & Elder, L. (2004). *The thinker's guide to the nature and functions of critical and creative thinking.* Dillon Beach, CA: Foundation for Critical Thinking.

Pfau, B. N., & Kay, I. T. (2002). *The human capital edge: Twenty-one people management practices your company must implement (or avoid) to maximize shareholder* value. New York: McGraw-Hill.

Popper, K. R. (1979). *Objective knowledge: An evolutionary approach.* Oxford: Clarendon Press.

Psacharopoulos, G. (1973). *Returns to education: An international comparison.* San Francisco: Jossey-Bass.

Psacharopoulos, G. (1975). *Earnings and education in OECD countries.* Paris: Organization for Economic Cooperation and Development.

Quinn, J. B., Anderson, P., & Finkelstein, S. (1996, March). Managing professional intellect: Making the most of the best. *Harvard Business Review, 72*(2), 71–82.

Quinn, R. E., Spreitzer, G. M., & Hart, S. (1992). Challenging the assumptions of bipolarity: Interpenetration and managerial effectiveness. In S. Srivastva & R. E. Fry (Eds.), *Executive and organizational continuity: Managing the paradoxes of stability and change.* San Francisco: Jossey-Bass.

Ritchie, D. (2004). Common ground in metaphor theory: Continuing the conversation. *Metaphor and Symbol, 19*(3), 233–44.

Robbins, H., & Finley, M. (2000). *The new why teams don't work: What goes wrong and how to make it right.* San Francisco: Berrett-Koehler.

Ruggiero, V. R. (1998). *The art of thinking: A guide to critical and creative thought* (5th ed.). New York: Addison Wesley Longman.

Samuelson, L. (2004, June). Modeling knowledge in economic analysis. *Journal of Economic Literature, 42*, 367–403.

Scarborough, N. M., & Zimmerer, T. W. (2000). *Effective small business management* (6th ed.). Upper Saddle River, NJ: Prentice-Hall.

Scheffler, I. (1965). *Conditions of knowledge.* Chicago: Scott, Foresman.

Schein, E. H. (2004). Innovative cultures and adaptive organizations. In M. L. Conner & J. G. Clawson (Eds.), *Creating a learning culture: strategy, technology, and practice* (pp. 123–51). Cambridge, UK: Cambridge University Press.

Schlosser, E. (2002). *Fast food nation: The dark side of the all-American meal.* New York: Harper Collins Perennial.

Schultz, T. W. (1961, March). Investment in human capital. *American Economic Review, 51*(1), 1–17.

Schuster, J. R., & Zingheim, P. K. (1992). *The new pay: Linking employee and organizational performance.* San Francisco: Jossey-Bass.

Senge, P. (1990). *The fifth discipline: The art and practice of the learning organization.* New York: Doubleday.

Shapiro, S. M. (2002). *24/7 innovation.* New York: McGraw-Hill.

Simon, H. A. (1980). Problem solving and education. In D. T. Tuma & R. Reif (Eds.), *Problem solving and education: Issues in teaching and research* (pp. 81–96). Hillsdale, NJ: Lawrence Erlbaum.

Smith, A. (1991). *The wealth of nations.* New York: Prometheus Books.

Spalding, J. L. (1901). Aphorisms and reflections: Conduct, culture and religion. In E. F. Murphy (Ed.), *Webster's Treasury of Relevant Quotations* (p. 1). New York: Granercy Books.

Spanyi, A., & Eibel-Spanyi, K. (2004, August). Nurturing innovation. *Strategic Finance, 86*(2), 25–29.

Stewart, T. A. (1999). *Intellectual capital: The new wealth of organizations.* New York: Currency Books–Doubleday.

Swartz, R. J., & Perkins, D. N. (1989). *Teaching thinking: Issues and approaches.* Pacific Grove, CA: Midwest Publications.

Teece, D. J. (1998). Capturing value from knowledge assets: The new economy, markets for know how, and intangible assets. *California Management Review, 40,* 55–79.

Tobin, D. R. (1998). *The knowledge-enabled organization: Moving from "training" to "learning" to meet business goals.* New York: AMACON.

Top Twenty Graduate Degrees. (2003, July–September). Retrieved June 3, 2004, from www.gradschools.com/archives/subjects.html.

Vygotsky, L. S. (1962). *Thought and language.* Cambridge, MA: MIT Press [originally published in 1934].

World Almanac and Book of Facts. (2003). New York: World Almanac Education Group.

World Bank. (1999). *World development report: Knowledge for development.* Oxford: Oxford University Press.

Yukl, G. A. (2002). *Leadership in organization* (5th ed.). Upper Saddle River, NJ: Prentice-Hall.

Zwart, D., & Resnick, H. S. (2000). *The ten things every training manager should know about TKM.* Golden, CO: Generation 21 Learning Systems.

INDEX

ABOUT THE AUTHOR

Roderic Hewlett is serving as the executive vice president and chief academic officer for Walsh College in Troy, Michigan. Dr. Hewlett's other academic appointments include professor and dean of the College of Business and Graduate School at Minot State University in Minot, North Dakota; associate professor and chair of business at the University of Dubuque, Dubuque, Iowa; and assistant professor of business at Clarke College in Dubuque, Iowa.

Hewlett earned his master's and doctorate degrees in economics at Middle Tennessee State University. He also earned the Certified Financial Manager and Certified Treasury Professional designations from the Association for Financial Professionals and Institute for Management Accountants, respectively. During his professional business career, he served in increasingly responsible professional and leadership positions at Northrop Corporation, Harris Corporation, Textron Corporation, Sundstrand Corporation, SABIC Corporation in Saudi Arabia, and the International Schools Group (ISG) in Saudi Arabia.

Dr. Hewlett is also a retired veteran after spending 26 years in the U.S. Army, serving in the regular and reserve forces, and now teaches as an adjunct professor in the executive MBA program at the Southwestern University of Finance and Economics located in Chengdu, China. He consults regularly with various governmental, business, and community organizations in the areas of strategic planning and development.